The Quotable Executive

Also in the *Quotable* Series:

The Quotable Writer by William A. Gordon
The Quotable Historian by Alan Axelrod
The Quotable Woman by Carol Turkington

The Quotable Executive

Words of Wisdom from Warren Buffett,
Jack Welch, Shelly Lazarus, Bill Gates,
Lou Gerstner, Richard Branson,
Carly Fiorina, Lee Iacocca, and more

John Woods

McGraw-Hill

New York San Francisco Washington, D.C. Auckland Bogotá
Caracas Lisbon London Madrid Mexico City Milan
Montreal New Delhi San Juan Singapore
Sydney Tokyo Toronto

McGraw-Hill

*A Division of The **McGraw·Hill** Companies*

1 2 3 4 5 6 7 8 9 0 DOC/DOC 0 9 8 7 6 5 4 3 2 1

ISBN 0-07-135734-3

This book was set in Berkeley by CWL Publishing Enterprises, Madison, WI, www.cwlpub.com. Printed and bound by R.R. Donnelly & Sons Company.

McGraw-Hill books are available at special quantity discounts to use as premiums and sales promotions, or for use in corporate training programs. For more information, please write to the Director of Special Sales, Professional Publishing, McGraw-Hill, Two Penn Plaza, New York, NY 10121-2298. Or contact your local bookstore.

 This book is printed on recycled, acid-free paper containing a minimum of 50% recycled, de-inked fiber.

Contents

Introduction

We are fascinated by quotes because they provide insight and capture in a few lines the essence of an issue. I have been collecting books of quotations for a long time. It's fun to read through them and get touched by a quote that puts a twist on a subject that I had not thought of before. It can jump-start our thinking in ways we hadn't considered. And when a person is looking for a way to enliven a speech or report, quotes work very well.

In this book, I have sought to give you quotations from a variety of sources, including thoughts from historical leaders mixed with the insights of past and contemporary business writers, consultants, and executives. Some of the quotations are directly applicable to life on the job, and others apply to life in general.

The topics here range from *action* to *attitude*, *big business* to *commitment*, *conflict* to *creativity*, and *enthusiasm* to *humility*. These are subjects that apply to us as human beings as well as workers. I hope, therefore, that when you're at work or at home, this little book will remind you that "the road to success is always under construction," and that "today's peacock is tomorrow's feather duster" and that "how you react when the joke's on you can reveal your character."

You can also learn that your ideas may be just as valid as those of leaders we read about in *Fast Company* or *Fortune*. Maybe reading the quotations in this book will encourage you to start keeping notes on your thoughts about management and performance. I certainly encourage you to do so. For a long time, I have been writing down my insights and thoughts, and, occasionally, you'll find those included here.

Thank you for choosing this book. I hope it meets your expectations. Enjoy!

John Woods

⌒ Acknowledgments ⌒

This collection of quotations would not have come together as well as it has without the help of three people, and I want to acknowledge their contributions. Vicky Jones spread a wide net, helping me run down quotations from many sources. Bob Magnan, who works with me at CWL Publishing Enterprises, is an editor extraordinaire, and he was responsible for helping me in many different ways, including proofreading and hunting down the identities of those whose words I have included here. Finally, my wife, Nancy Woods, also read the final pages and made suggestions for improvement.

I also want to thank my editor at McGraw-Hill, Nancy Mikhail, who suggested I do this book. I appreciate her support throughout the project. And to you, the reader, I want to say thanks for buying this book. I hope it stimulates your thinking and helps you to see that the principles of business management and the principles of living with reason and with passion are essentially the same.

Ability

Just do what you do best.

— RED AUERBACH, **former coach, Boston Celtics**

Ability is of little account without opportunity.

— NAPOLEON BONAPARTE, **former emperor of France**

No amount of ability is of the slightest avail without honor.

— ANDREW CARNEGIE, **founder, U.S. Steel**

The first requisite for success is the ability to apply your physical and mental energies to one problem incessantly without growing weary.

— THOMAS A. EDISON, **American inventor**

It is all one to me if a man comes from Sing Sing Prison or Harvard. We hire a man, not his history.

— HENRY FORD, **founder, Ford Motor Company**

Ability will never catch up with the demand for it.

— MALCOLM S. FORBES, **former publisher, *Forbes* magazine**

There is something that is much more scarce, something rarer than ability. It is the ability to recognize ability.

— ROBERT HALF, **founder, Robert Half International**

The greatest ability in business is to get along with others and influence their actions.

— JOHN HANCOCK, **signer, Declaration of Independence**

I won't accept anything less than the best a player's capable of doing ... and he has the right to expect the best that I can do for him and the team!

— LOU HOLTZ, **football coach, University of South Carolina**

Ability hits the mark where presumption overshoots and diffidence falls short.
— JOHN HENRY NEWMAN, Anglican and Roman Catholic theologian and Cardinal

Do not let what you cannot do interfere with what you can do.
— JOHN WOODEN, former basketball coach, UCLA

Accounting

[A sound accounting system] not only reveals our mistakes—it shows us what a good job we're doing.
— BROR R. CARLSON, director of accounting, International Minerals & Chemical Co.

One of the chief sources of success in manufacturing is the introduction and strict maintenance of a perfect system of accounting so that responsibility for money or materials can be brought home to every man.
— ANDREW CARNEGIE, founder, U.S. Steel

The higher mind has no need to concern itself with the meticulous regimentation of figures.
— WINSTON CHURCHILL, former Prime Minister, Great Britain

Many financial measurements which are useful and valid in steady-state or static situations are strategic traps in growth situations.
— BRUCE HENDERSON, former CEO, Boston Consulting Group

An accountant is a man who puts his head in the past and backs his ass into the future.
— ROSS JOHNSON, former CEO, RJR Nabisco

Today's management accounting information, driven by the procedures and cycle of the organization's financial reporting system, is too late, too aggregated, and too distorted to be relevant for managers' planning and control decisions.

— THOMAS H. JOHNSON AND ROBERT L. KAPLAN, authors, *Relevance Lost*

It's easier to teach a poet how to read a balance sheet than it is to teach an accountant how to write.

— HENRY R. LUCE, founder, Time Life

If the businessman would stop talking like a computer printout or a page from the corporate annual report, other people would stop thinking he had a cash register for a heart. It is as simple as that— but that isn't simple.

— LOUIS B. LUNDBORG (1906-1981), U.S. banker

[W]e like to depreciate as much as possible even though we sacrifice our profits the first year.... We were very much surprised that American management does not want to have such a fast depreciation because, as an American partner told me, he did not want to sacrifice his profit to his successor.

— AKIO MORITA, former CEO, Sony Corp.

We don't have a staff of business analysts in our headquarters.... Those financial people can only crunch numbers. They can't add any original thinking.

— ROBERT PRITZKER, president, Marmon Group

Creativity is great—but not in accounting.

— CHARLES SCOTT, CEO, Intermark

I don't know any CEO who doesn't love numbers.

— JEFFREY SILVERMAN, CEO, PlyGem Industries Ltd.

Businesses always have problems. Numbers tell you where the problems are and how worried you should be.

—JACK STACK, CEO, Springfield Remanufacturing Corporation, and author, *The Great Game of Business*

A good part of the problem [poor productivity] ... lies with the current accounting system, which sort of makes overhead disappear—it simply gets added into the cost of a product, like a tax.

—PAUL STRASSMANN, former VP, Xerox, and business author

While the total US economic output rose only 15 percent from 1978 to 1985, the number of accountants on corporate staffs increased by 30 percent.

—LESTER THUROW, former dean, MIT Sloan School of Business

Achievement

A state of statistical control is not a natural state for a process; it is an achievement.

—W. EDWARDS DEMING, consultant and author, *Out of the Crisis*

Somehow I can't believe that there are any heights that can't be scaled by a man who knows the secrets of making dreams come true. This special secret, it seems to me, can be summarized in four C's. They are curiosity, confidence, courage, and constancy, and the greatest of all is confidence.

—WALT DISNEY, founder, The Walt Disney Company

The three great essentials to achieve anything worthwhile are, first, hard work; second, stick-to-itiveness, third, common sense.

—THOMAS A. EDISON, American inventor

Too many of us, when we accomplish what we set out to do, exclaim, "See what I have done!" instead of saying, "See where I have been led."
—HENRY FORD, founder, Ford Motor Company

A man is the sum of his actions, of what he has done, of what he can do. Nothing else.
—MOHANDAS K. GANDHI, leader, Indian independence movement

Everyone has superstitions. One of mine has always been when I started to go anywhere, or to do anything, never to turn back or to stop until the thing intended was accomplished.
—ULYSSES S. GRANT, Civil War general and 17th U.S. President

The starting point of all achievement is desire. Keep this constantly in mind. Weak desires bring weak results, just as a small amount of fire makes a small amount of heat.
—NAPOLEON HILL, author, *Think and Grow Rich*

I've never known a man worth his salt who in the long run, deep down in his heart, didn't appreciate the grind, the discipline… I firmly believe that any man's finest hour—this greatest fulfillment to all he holds dear—is that moment when he has worked his heart out in a good cause and lies exhausted on the field of battle victorious.
—VINCE LOMBARDI, legendary coach, Green Bay Packers

The roots of true achievement lie in the will to become the best that you can become.
—HAROLD TAYLOR, author, *Harold Taylor Time Tips*, founder of Harold Taylor Time Consultants, Inc.

Look at a day when you are supremely satisfied at the end. It's not a day when you lounge around doing nothing; it's when you've had everything to do, and you've done it.
—MARGARET THATCHER, former Prime Minister, Great Britain

The outstanding leaders of every age are those who set up their own quotas and constantly exceed them.
—THOMAS J. WATSON, SR., founder, IBM

Action

I must not rust.
—CLARA BARTON, founder, Red Cross

Take time to deliberate, but when the time for action has arrived, stop thinking and go in.
—NAPOLEON BONAPARTE, former emperor of France

This is as true in everyday life as it is in battle: we are given one life and the decision is ours whether to wait for circumstances to make up our mind, or whether to act and, in acting, to live.
—OMAR BRADLEY, World War II general

Someone's sitting in the shade today because someone planted a tree a long time ago.
—WARREN BUFFET, CEO, Berkshire Hathaway

I see myself as a doer. I'm sure that other people have had ideas that were similar to mine. The difference is that I have carried mine into action, and they have not.
—NOLAN BUSHNELL, founder, Atari

I never worry about action, but only inaction.
—WINSTON CHURCHILL, former Prime Minister, Great Britain

The maxim, "Nothing prevails but perfection," may be spelled PARALYSIS.
— WINSTON CHURCHILL, former Prime Minister, Great Britain

Action may not always bring happiness, but there is no happiness without.
— BENJAMIN DISRAELI, 19th century Prime Minister, Great Britain

The victors of the battles of tomorrow will be those who can best harness thought to action.
— B.C. FORBES, founder, *Forbes* magazine

What if Columbus had been told, "Chris, baby, don't go now. Wait until we've solved our number-one priorities—war and famine; poverty and crime; pollution and disease; illiteracy and racial hatred...."
— BILL GATES, chairman and cofounder, Microsoft

We know the mistake of doing nothing from our own experience.
— MIKHAIL GORBACHEV, former President, USSR

Indecision is an insult to progress. When it's time to make a decision about a person or problem... trust your intuition... act!
— BUD HADFIELD, founder, Kwik Kopy

Success seems to be connected with action. Successful men keep moving. They make mistakes, but they don't quit.
— CONRAD HILTON, founder, Hilton Hotels

So what do we do? Anything. Something. So long as we just don't sit there. If we screw it up, start over. Try something else. If we wait until we've satisfied all the uncertainties, it may be too late.
— LEE IACOCCA, former chairman, Chrysler Corp.

Both tears and sweat are salty, but they render a different result. Tears will get you sympathy; sweat will get you change.
—JESSE JACKSON, U.S. civil rights leader

You will never stub your toe standing still. The faster you go, the more chance there is of stubbing your toe, but the more chance you have of getting somewhere.
—CHARLES F. KETTERING, president, General Motors Research Corp., and cofounder, Sloan-Kettering Institute for Cancer Research

You can't pick cherries with your back to the tree.
—J. PIERPONT MORGAN, American financier

Action to be effective must be directed to clearly conceived ends.
—JAWAHARLAL NEHRU, first Prime Minister, India

Just do it.
—NIKE CORPORATION

Act like you expect to get into the end zone.
—JOE PATERNO, football coach, Penn State University

The activist is not the man who says the river is dirty. The activist is the man who cleans up the river.
—H. ROSS PEROT, founder, EDS and Perot Systems

Either move or be moved.
—COLIN POWELL, general and former head, Joint Chiefs of Staff

You prove your worth with your actions, not with your mouth.
—PAT RILEY, coach, Miami Heat professional basketball team

When you see a rattlesnake poised to strike you, do not wait until he has struck before you crush him.
—FRANKLIN D. ROOSEVELT, U.S. President

Whoever wants to reach a distant goal must take small steps.

　　—HELMUT SCHMIDT, **former Prime Minister, Germany**

The truth of the matter is that you always know the right thing to do. The hard part is doing it.

　　—NORMAN SCHWARZKOPF, **general, commander, Gulf War**

The greatest of all mistakes is to do nothing because you can only do a little. Do what you can.

　　—SYDNEY SMITH, **19th century English clergyman and cofounder of the *Edinburgh Review***

Try not. Do, or do not. There is no try.

　　—YODA, **Jedi master**

Advertising

If advertising had a little more respect for the public, the public would have a lot more respect for advertising.

　　—JAMES RANDOLPH ADAMS, **cofounder and president, McManus, John & Adams, Inc.**

No company that markets products or services to the consumer can remain a leader in its field without a deep-seated commitment to advertising.

　　—EDWIN L. ARTZT, **former CEO, Procter & Gamble**

The faults of advertising are only these common to all human institutions. If advertising speaks to a thousand in order to influence one, so does the church. And if it encourages people to live beyond their means, so does matrimony.

　　—BRUCE BARTON, **cofounder, BBDO Advertising**

A great ad campaign will make a bad product fail faster. It will get more people to know it's bad.
—WILLIAM BERNBACH, cofounder, DDB Needham Advertising

Just because your ad looks good is no insurance that it will get looked at. How many people do you know who are impeccably groomed ... but dull?
—WILLIAM BERNBACH

When a man throws an empty cigarette package from an automobile, he is liable to a fine of $50. When a man throws a billboard across a view, he is richly rewarded.
—PAT BROWN, former Governor of California

The sole purpose of business is service. The sole purpose of advertising is explaining the service which business renders.
—LEO BURNETT, founder, Leo Burnett Advertising

We want consumers to say, "That's a hell of a product," instead of, "That's a hell of an ad."
—LEO BURNETT

Advertising promotes that divine discontent which makes people strive to improve their economic status.
—RALPH STARR BUTLER, vice president of advertising, General Foods, and author of *Marketing Methods* (1917)

Asked about the power of advertising in research surveys, most agree that it works, but not on them.
—PERIC CLARK, author, *Inside the World of Advertising*

Advertising is what you do when you can't go see somebody.
—FAIRFAX CONE, former CEO, Foote Cone & Belding Advertising

Make the layouts rough and the ideas fancy.
—STAVROS COSMOPULOS, Cosmopulos Creative Services

There are quite a few votes to be won by saying we will tax advertising or stop it.

    —BARRY DAY, vice chairman, McCann Erickson Advertising

I honestly believe that advertising is the most fun you can have with your clothes on.

    —JERRY DELLA FEMINA, cofounder, Della Femina, Travisano & Partners

That's the kind of ad I like: facts, facts, facts.

    —SAMUEL GOLDWYN, cofounder, Metro-Goldwyn-Mayer Studios

You see, advertising is a substitute for a salesperson, so it should be likeable. Who would buy from a salesperson who is rude, arrogant or insulting? People like to do business with people they like, therefore they respond to advertising created by people who like people.

    —JERRY GOODIS, cofounder, Goodis, Goldberg, Dair advertising agency

Nobody reads advertising. People read what interests them, and sometimes it's an ad.

    —HOWARD LUCK GOSSAGE, cofounder of Weiner & Gossage, Freeman & Gossage and Freeman, and Mander & Gossage advertising agencies

In the past, we have had a strategy, but our agencies didn't stick to it. But they did make good commercials and they did win awards. This may surprise you, though. I don't care about awards; I want to sell product.

    —JAMES W. HARRALSON, CEO, Royal Crown Cola

Advertising is salesmanship mass produced. No one would bother to use advertising if he could talk to all his prospects face to face. But he can't.

    —MORRIS HITE, chair 1950-1982, Tracy-Locke advertising agency (now DDB Needham)

Young people are threatened ... by the evil use of advertising techniques that stimulate the natural inclination to avoid hard work by promising the immediate satisfaction of every desire.
— POPE JOHN PAUL II

Advertising is any communication that seeks to influence, persuade, inform or educate the consumer—any commercial message about the brand that touches the consumer. That's advertising.
— SHELLY LAZARUS, chairman, Ogilvy & Mather Advertising

Advertising may be described as the science of arresting the human intelligence long enough to get money from it.
— STEPHEN LEACOCK, economist

If it doesn't sell, it isn't creative.
— DAVID OGILVY, cofounder, Ogilvy & Mather Advertising

The more informative your advertising, the more persuasive it will be.
— DAVID OGILVY

When executing advertising, it's best to think of yourself as an uninvited guest in the living room of a prospect who has the magical power to make you disappear instantly.
— JOHN O'TOOLE, chairman, Foote Cone & Belding

Political commercials encourage the deceptive, the destructive and the degrading.
— JOHN O'TOOLE

Advertising is [a] ten billion dollar a year misunderstanding with the public.
— CHESTER L. POSEY, senior V.P. and creative director, McCann Erickson

I wish all consumers were as gullible as advertising's biggest critics. Anyone who believes advertising is that powerful will believe almost anything.
— JEF I. RICHARDS, advertising professor, University of Texas

The value of an ad is in inverse ratio to the number of times it has been used.

➤RAYMOND RUBICAM, founder, Young & Rubicam Advertising

Advertising is a non-moral force, like electricity, which not only illuminates but electrocutes. Its worth to civilization depends upon how it is used.

➤J. WALTER THOMPSON, founder, J. Walter Thompson Advertising

I know half the money I spend on advertising is wasted, but I can never find out which half.

➤JOHN WANAMAKER, founder, Wanamaker Department Stores

 *Advice*

Ineffective leaders often act on the advice and counsel of the last person they talked to.

➤WARREN BENNIS, founder and chair of the Leadership Institute, University of Southern California

Wall Street in the only place that people ride to in a Rolls Royce to get advice from those who take the subway.

➤WARREN BUFFET, CEO, Berkshire Hathaway

Advice: It's more fun to give than to receive.

➤MALCOLM FORBES, former publisher, *Forbes* magazine

Listening to advice often accomplishes far more than heeding it.

➤MALCOLM FORBES

"Be yourself" is the worst advice you can give some people.

➤TOM MASSON, essayist (1866-1934)

In his heart everyone knows that the only people who get rich from the *get rich quick* books are those who write them.
　　—RICHARD M. NIXON, U.S. President

You don't need to take a person's advice to make him feel good— just ask for it.
　　—LAURENCE J. PETER, author, *The Peter Principle*

I've found that the best way to give advice to your children is to find out what they want and then advise them to do it.
　　—HARRY S. TRUMAN, U.S. President

Agreement

Do not trust to the cheering, for those persons would shout as much if you and I were going to be hanged.
　　—OLIVER CROMWELL, Lord Protector of England, 1653-1658

Honest disagreement is often a good sign of progress.
　　—MOHANDAS K. GANDHI, leader, Indian independence movement

If two men agree on everything, you may be sure that one of them is doing the thinking.
　　—LYNDON B. JOHNSON, U.S. President

If we are all in agreement on the decision ..., then I propose we postpone further discussion of this matter until our next meeting to give ourselves time to develop disagreement and perhaps gain some understanding of what the decision is all about.
　　—ALFRED P. SLOAN, JR., president and CEO, General Motors, 1923-1946

When two men in business always agree, one of them is unnecessary.

    —WILLIAM WRIGLEY, JR., founder, William Wrigley Jr. Company

Ambition

Very few people are ambitious in the sense of having a specific image of what they want to achieve. Most people's sights are only toward the next run, the next increment of money.

    —JUDITH M. BARDWICK, president, Bardwick & Associates, management consulting firm

I don't try to jump over seven-foot bars. I look around for one-foot bars that I can step over.

    —WARREN BUFFET, CEO, Berkshire Hathaway

When you reach for the stars, you may not quite get one, but you won't come up with a handful of mud either.

    —LEO BURNETT, founder, Leo Burnett Advertising

I would rather be first in a little Iberian village than second in Rome.

    —JULIUS CAESAR, Roman emperor

Big results require big ambitions.

    —JAMES CHAMPY, chairman, Perot Systems Consulting

I do not like to repeat success, I like to go on to other things.

    —WALT DISNEY, founder, The Walt Disney Company

When you catch what you're after, it's gone.

    —MALCOLM FORBES, former publisher, *Forbes* magazine

In the business world, everyone is always working at legitimate cross purposes, governed by self-interest.
—HAROLD GENEEN, former CEO, IT&T

I cannot honestly claim that I possessed any innate talent nor even any particular desire for a business career.
—J. PAUL GETTY, founder, Getty Oil

Sure, I had opportunities to run a start-up. But money isn't the big motivator for me. What I'm really motivated by is the opportunity to run a huge friggin' business.
—DANIEL HAMBURGER, vice president, Grainger Internet Commerce

You are ambitious, which within reasonable bounds, does good rather than harm.
—ABRAHAM LINCOLN, U.S. President

Ambition is so powerful a passion in the human breast, that however high we reach we are never satisfied.
—NICCOLO MACHIAVELLI, author, *The Prince*

I had no ambition to make a fortune. Mere money-making has never been my goal. I had an ambition to build.
—JOHN D. ROCKEFELLER, JR., U.S. oil magnate and philanthropist

When a man has put a limit on what he will do, he has put a limit on what he can do.
—CHARLES M. SCHWAB, former CEO, Bethlehem Steel

One only gets to the top rung on the ladder by steadily climbing up one at a time, and suddenly all sorts of powers, all sorts of abilities which you thought never belonged to you—suddenly become within your own possibility and you think, "Well, I'll have a go too."
—MARGARET THATCHER, former Prime Minister, Great Britain

Don't let ambitions for what you want to do tomorrow get in the way of doing what you are supposed to do today.

➤ JOHN WOODS, **president, CWL Publishing Enterprises**

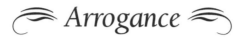

Arrogance

Every man has a right to his opinion, but no man has a right to be wrong in his facts.

➤ BERNARD BARUCH, **American financier and presidential advisor**

Companies which get misled by their own success are sure to be blindsided.

➤ WARREN BENNIS, **founder and chair, Leadership Institute, University of Southern California**

Dictators ride to and fro upon tigers which they dare not dismount, and the tigers are getting hungry.

➤ WINSTON CHURCHILL, **former Prime Minister, Great Britain**

We live in a world where corporate executives believe they can spend the assets of … corporations for their own creature comforts. Those executives … have created a high flying world of undisclosed corporate jets, corporate apartments, hunting lodges, country clubs, and martini infused lunches, all unwarranted and all paid for by unknowing shareholders.

➤ ASHER B. EDELMAN, **partner, Plaza Securities**

Anyone who tends toward arrogance, as I do, should be sentenced to a term of venture capital fund-raising during a tight market.

➤ CHARLES H. FERGUSON, **founder, Vermeer Technologies**

The man who is smugly confident that he has arrived is ripe for the return trip. A measure of self confidence is an asset when you are battling your way to the top. But cocksuredness is not an asset but a liability. It tends to dull the edge of effort. Also, it breeds arrogance that is distasteful.

—B.C. FORBES, founder, *Forbes* magazine

Are you not justified in feeling inferior, when you seek to cover it up with arrogance and insolence?

—MALCOLM FORBES, former publisher, *Forbes* magazine

The worst disease which can afflict executives in their work is not, as popularly supposed, alcoholism; it's egotism.

—HAROLD S. GENEEN, former CEO, IT&T

Bury your ego. Don't be the star. Be the star maker!

—BUD HADFIELD, founder, Kwik Kopy

Ego trip: a journey to nowhere.

—ROBERT HALF, founder, Robert Half International

It's a dangerous thing to think we know everything.

—JACK KUEHLER, former vice chairman, IBM

When a client comes to us with a product, he is, in effect, giving us a problem to be solved.... Some of the biggest advertising mistakes are people who imagine they know what the problem is, or they're not even thinking about it; they're just coming up with that brilliant idea and trying to force the problem to fit it.

—MARY WELLS LAWRENCE, cofounder, Wells, Rich & Greene Advertising

We had been a proud group who felt that people who knew nothing were telling us what to do. It took us a long time to realize that regulators, legislators, even environmentalists have a right to ask questions.

—KEITH R. MCKENNON, president, Dow Chemical

All silencing of discussion is an assumption of infallibility.
—JOHN STUART MILL, **economist**

Managers tend to make their biggest mistakes in things they've previously done best. In business, as elsewhere, hubris is the unforgivable sin of acting cocky when things are going well. As the Greeks tiresomely told us, Hubris is followed inexorably and inevitably by Nemesis.
—ROBERT TOWNSEND, **former CEO, Avis Rent-a-Car, and author,** *Up the Organization*

Aspiration

He who stops being better, stops being good.
—OLIVER CROMWELL, **Lord Protector of England, 1653-1658**

Show me a thoroughly satisfied man—and I will show you a failure.
—THOMAS A. EDISON, **American inventor**

We'd all like to be taken for what we'd like to be.
—MALCOLM FORBES, **former publisher,** *Forbes* **magazine**

You must be the change you wish to see in the world.
—MOHANDAS K. GANDHI, **leader, Indian independence movement**

The hallmark of our age is the tension between aspirations and sluggish institutions.
—JOHN GARDNER, **founder, Common Cause**

I always have to dream up there against the stars. If I don't dream I'll make it, I won't even get close.
—HENRY J. KAISER, **founder, Kaiser Steel**

The greatest role that life can bestow upon you is to be a revolutionary.

— GUY KAWASAKI, former evangelist, Apple, CEO, garage.com, and author, *Rules for Revolutionaries*, *Selling the Dream*, and *How to Drive Your Competition Crazy*

I refuse to accept the idea that the "isness" of man's present nature makes him morally incapable of reaching up for the "oughtness" that forever confronts him.

— MARTIN LUTHER KING, JR., American civil rights leader

Don't bunt. Aim out of the ball park. Aim for the company of immortals.

— DAVID OGILVY, cofounder, Ogilvy & Mather Advertising

Keep your eyes on the stars and your feet on the ground.

— THEODORE ROOSEVELT, U.S. President

Whatever you want in life, other people are going to want it too. Believe in yourself enough to accept the idea that you have an equal right to it.

— DIANE SAWYER, U.S. broadcast journalist

Dreams never hurt anybody if you keep working right behind the dreams to make as much of them become real as you can.

— FRANK W. WOOLWORTH, founder, F.W. Woolworth Stores

 *Attitude*

You can overcome anything if you don't bellyache.

— BERNARD BARUCH, American financier and presidential advisor

There are no menial jobs, only menial attitudes.

— WILLIAM BENNETT, former U.S. Secretary of Education

Did you ever see an unhappy horse? Did you ever see a bird that had the blues? One reason why birds and horses are not unhappy is because they are not trying to impress other birds and horses.

　━DALE CARNEGIE, author, *How to Win Friends and Influence People*

A pessimist sees the difficulty in every opportunity; an optimist sees the opportunity in every difficulty.

　━WINSTON CHURCHILL, former Prime Minister, Great Britain

I don't think anything is unrealistic if you believe you can do it.

　━MIKE DITKA, professional football coach

What happens is not as important as how you react to what happens.

　━THADDEUS GOLAS, author, *Lazy Man's Guide to Enlightenment*

Nothing gives one person so much advantage over another as to remain cool and unruffled under all circumstances.

　━THOMAS JEFFERSON, U.S. President

My attitude is never to be satisfied, never enough, never.

　━BELA KAROLYI, Olympics gymnastics coach

In order to succeed, we must first believe that we can.

　━MICHAEL KORDA, author, *Power! How to Get It, How to Use It*

Most people are about as happy as they make up their minds to be.

　━ABRAHAM LINCOLN, U.S. President

The spirit, the will to win, and the will to excel are the things that endure. These qualities are so much more important than the events that occur.

　━VINCE LOMBARDI, legendary coach, Green Bay Packers

As usual, the serious me is working hard, but the real me is having fun.

　━JOHN REED, CEO, Citicorp

Don't be against things so much as for things.
— COLONEL HARLAN SANDERS, founder, Kentucky Fried Chicken Restaurants

This is the precept by which I have lived: Prepare for the worst; expect the best; and take what comes.
— ROBERT E. SPEER, secretary of the Presbyterian Board of Foreign Missions for 46 years

There is little difference in people, but that little difference makes a big difference. That little difference is attitude. The big difference is whether it is positive or negative.
— W. CLEMENT STONE, author, *Think and Grow Rich*

Being broke is a temporary situation. Being poor is a state of mind.
— MIKE TODD, American movie producer

Celebrate your success and find humor in your failures. Don't take yourself so seriously. Loosen up and everyone around you will loosen up. Have fun and always show enthusiasm. When all else fails put on a costume and sing a silly song.
— SAM WALTON, founder, Wal-Mart

I've learned from experience that the greater part of our happiness or misery depends on our dispositions and not on our circumstances.
— MARTHA WASHINGTON, first First Lady

Authority

Dear, never forget one little point: It's my business. You just work here.
— ELIZABETH ARDEN, founder, Elizabeth Arden Cosmetics

Nothing more advances authority than silence.
　—CHARLES DE GAULLE, former President, France

Those who enjoy responsibility usually get it; those who merely like exercising authority usually lose it.
　—MALCOLM FORBES, former publisher, *Forbes* magazine

I don't believe in ordering people to do things. You have to sort of grab an oar and row with them.
　—HAROLD GENEEN, former CEO, IT&T

Authority poisons everybody who takes authority on himself.
　—VLADIMIR ILYICH LENIN, leader, Russian Revolution

No man is good enough to govern another man without that other man's consent.
　—ABRAHAM LINCOLN, U.S. President

A boss's mere expression of an opinion can be interpreted as a decision—even a direct order—by a staff member caught in the clutches of risk avoidance.
　—R. ALEC MACKENZIE, consultant and author, *The Time Trap* and other books

My way or the highway.
　—BARRY MINKOW, former head of ZZZZ BEST Carpet Cleaning, now senior pastor at Community Bible Church, Mira Mesa, Calif.

News is what your city editor says it is.
　—JOHN H. SORRELLS, managing editor, The Cleveland Press, 1920s

Strange as it sounds, great leaders gain authority by giving it away.
　—JAMES B. STOCKDALE, vice admiral, POW, Vietnam War

Big Business

It is such a delight now [that I'm not working for a large corporation] to make decisions based on one criterion only; is it a good decision, in both the short term and the long term?
— CHARLES J. BODENSTAB, author, consultant, seminar leader, and executive vice president of Data Systems and Management, Inc.

If a company gets too large, break it into smaller parts. Once people start not knowing the people in the building and it starts to become impersonal, it's time to break up a company.
— RICHARD BRANSON, founder, Virgin Group

The more common pattern [of business innovation] is that the ideas are developed by smaller companies that get to the point where they need more money, and they get bought by the larger companies.
— LAUREL CUTLER, vice chairman, FCB/Leber Katz Partners

We have always found that, if our principles were right, the area over which they were applied did not matter. Size is only a matter of the multiplication table.
— HENRY FORD, founder, Ford Motor Co.

Size works against excellence.
— BILL GATES, founder and chairman, Microsoft

Going to work for a large company is like getting on a train. Are you going sixty miles an hour, or is the train going sixty miles an hour and you're just sitting still?
— J. PAUL GETTY, founder, Getty Oil

Economy, stability, and absence of friction are striking characteristics of large corporations.
— KING GILLETTE, founder, Gillette Razor

A big corporation is more or less blamed for being big. It is only big because it gives service. If it doesn't give service, it gets small faster than it grew big.

— William S. Knudsen, former president, General Motors

Humans are creative, fun and inquiring; yet work for so many is monotonous, complex and dreary. Humans are individual and versatile; yet at work we discover we are all expendable and carefully placed in a well-manicured organogram.

— Andy Law, chairman, St. Luke's Advertising

Big business breeds bureaucracy and bureaucrats act exactly as big government does.

— Theodore K. Quinn, head of General Electric Electric Refrigeration Department, late 1920s and early 1930s, and author, *Giant Business, Threat to Democracy, The Autobiography of an Insider*

Continued frustration with the intransigence of large corporations—their reluctance to promote women more aggressively or to adopt more family-friendly policies—will prompt women to look for even more radical ways to bring about economic equality.

— Nancy Ramsey, president, Morning Star Imports

Sometimes I am almost forced to the conclusion that General Motors is so large and its inertia so great that it is impossible for us to be leaders.

— Alfred P. Sloan, Jr., president and CEO, General Motors, 1923-1946

Large organizations can't tolerate constant turmoil.

— Philip Smith, chairman, General Foods

Where is all this great stuff coming from? It's coming out of little two and three man companies, because they're finding out that forty guys can't do something that three people can do. It's just the law of human nature.

— Roger Smith, former chairman, General Motors

Bigger organizations spend too much time and overhead on internal communications.

—JIM SWIGGERT, CEO, Kollmorgen Corp.

Big companies are small companies that succeeded.

—ROBERT TOWNSEND, former CEO, Avis Rent-a-Car, and author, *Up the Organization*

What is good for the country is good for General Motors, and vice versa.

—CHARLES E. WILSON, former CEO, General Motors, and Secretary of Defense in the Eisenhower administration

Brands

Any company that tried to get by with unconnected and directionless local brand strategies will inevitably find mediocrity as its reward.

—DAVID A. AAKER AND ERICK JOACHIMSTHALER, marketing authors and researchers, University of California, Berkeley

Brand loyalty is very much like an onion. It has layers and a core. The core is the user who will stick with you until the very end.

—EDWIN ARTZT, former CEO, Procter & Gamble

How can you, your people, your products—and therefore your brand—create a human connection? Or, to put it differently, now that everyone's bragging about their brand, how can a product develop humility?

—SCOTT BEDBURY, consultant and author, *A New Brand World*

I'll tell you why I like the cigarette business. It costs a penny to make. Sell it for a dollar. It's addictive. And there's a fantastic brand loyalty.

— WARREN BUFFET, CEO, Berkshire Hathaway

Consumers build brands like birds build nests, from scraps and straws they chance upon.

— JEREMY BULLMORE, executive, J. Walter Thompson

To me, branding is the new buzzword because companies are not willing to buy products just for the sake of the product... Unfortunately, there are a lot of folks out there who really don't have soul, but who are doing this branding thing as a way to stay alive. All that does it to dilute what is authentic about branding.

— LAURIE COOT, chief marketing officer, TBWA/Chiat/Day

One of the toughest problems with brands today is that success breeds failure. Ingrained in every consumer is a sensibility that roots for the underdog.... Which is why I don't buy Nikes anymore. Products get to a point where, all of a sudden, they're no longer cool.

— TIM DEMELLO, CEO, Streamline

A brand signals a set of expectations and a core understanding that drives everything.

— SHELLY LAZARUS, chairman and CEO, Ogilvy & Mather Advertising

You build your brand by communicating it 360 degrees in every way that you can, in every point of contact with the many groups that touch your brand, all your audiences, all your relationships.

— SHELLY LAZARUS

You cannot sustainably change an identity unless it fits with reality.

— GEOFF MULGAN, founder and director of Demos, an independent think tank based in London

Nobody has ever built a brand by imitating somebody else's advertising.

━DAVID OGILVY, cofounder, Ogilvy & Mather Advertising

Today brands are everything, and all kinds of products and services—from accounting firms to sneaker makers to restaurants—are figuring out how to transcend the narrow boundaries of their categories and become a brand surrounded by a Tommy Hilfiger-like buzz.

━TOM PETERS, author and consultant

In the old days, first you'd create a product, then you'd build a brand around it. In the new paradigm it's the other way around: The product is driven by the brand.

━NICK SHORE, managing director, Enterprise IG, brand and identity consultants

Most people can't understand what would drive someone to profess his or her loyalty for our brand by tattooing our logo onto his or her body or heart.

━RICHARD TEERLINK, former CEO, Harley-Davidson

One of the benefits of branding is brand equity. If we build brand equity, there is an umbrella for the product to operate under. That can carry you through good and bad times.

━STRAUSS ZELNICK, president and CEO, BMG Entertainment

Bureaucracy

One of the enduring truths of the nation's capital is that bureaucrats survive.

━GERALD FORD, U.S. President

Hell has no fury like a bureaucrat scorned.

━MILTON FRIEDMAN, economist

Over-seriousness is a warning sign for mediocrity and bureaucratic thinking. People who are seriously committed to mastery and high performance are secure enough to lighten up.

    —MICHAEL J. GELB, **author, books on creativity**

Company success is inverse to the deployment of PowerPoint.

    —BILL GROSS, **chairman, idealab!**

I would rather be exposed to the inconveniences attending too much liberty than those attending too small a degree of it.

    —THOMAS JEFFERSON, **U.S. President**

The only thing that saves us from the bureaucracy is its inefficiency.

    —EUGENE MCCARTHY, **former U.S. Senator and presidential candidate**

If we did not have such a thing as an airplane today, we would probably create something the size of NASA to make one.

    —H. ROSS PEROT, **founder, EDS and Perot Systems**

The first EDSer to see a snake kills it. At GM, the first thing you do is organize a committee on snakes. Then you bring in a consultant who knows a lot about snakes. Third thing you do is talk about it for a year.

    —H. ROSS PEROT

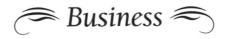

Business

Commerce is the most important activity on the face of the earth. It is the foundation on which civilization is built. Religion, society, education—all have their roots in business, and would have to be reorganized in their material aspects should business fail.

    —JAMES RANDOLPH ADAMS, **cofounder and president, McManus, John & Adams, Inc.**

The fundamental principles that govern the handling of a few postage stamps and millions of dollars are exactly the same. They are so simple that a fool can learn them; so hard that a lazy man won't.
— PHILIP D. ARMOUR, founder, Armour & Co.

Business is really more agreeable than pleasure; it interests the whole mind, the aggregate nature of man more continuously, and more deeply. But it does not look as if it did.
— WALTER BAGEHOT, founding editor, *The Economist*

In war, the stronger overcomes the weaker. In business, the stronger imparts strength to the weaker.
— FREDERIC BASTIAT, 19th century French economist

If you can run one business well, you can run any business well.
— RICHARD BRANSON, founder, Virgin Group

Business has only two functions—marketing and innovation.
— PETER F. DRUCKER, consultant and renowned management author

To supply the wants and needs of a consumer, society entrusts wealth-producing resources to the business enterprise.
— PETER F. DRUCKER

There is one rule for industrialists and that is: Make the best quality of goods possible at the lowest cost possible paying the highest wages possible.
— HENRY FORD, founder, Ford Motor Company

Business is ... a fluid, ever changing, living thing, sometimes building to great peaks, sometimes falling to crumbled lumps. The soul of a business is a curious alchemy of needs, desires, greed and gratifications mixed together with selflessness, sacrifices and personal contributions far beyond material needs.
— HAROLD GENEEN, former CEO, IT&T

I believe that the able industrial leader who creates wealth and employment is more worthy of historical notice than politicians or soldiers.

— J. Paul Getty, founder, Getty Oil

It is as if all America were but a giant workshop, over the entrance of which is the blazing inscription, "No admission here, except on business."

— F. J. (Francis Joseph) Grund, diplomat, journalist, and author, *The Americans in their Moral, Social and Political Relations* (1837) and *Aristocracy in America* (1839)

Part of the economy dies every day and is replaced by something new.

— Paul Hawken, cofounder, Smith & Hawken

We have to be as tough as, if not tougher than our competitors. I don't want anybody to pat me on the head or to give us a contract because we're nice. We earn the business we get.

— Eleanor Josaitis, founder, Focus:Hope, a Detroit development organization

In business, the competition will bite you if you keep running; if you stand still, they will swallow you.

— William S. Knudsen, former president, General Motors

Business, more than any other occupation, is a continual dealing with the future; it is a continual calculation, an instinctive exercise in foresight.

— Henry Luce, founder, Time Life

The secret of business is to know something that nobody else knows.

— Aristotle Onassis, Greek ship owner and financier

To succeed in business it is necessary to make others see things as you see them.

— JOHN H. PATTERSON, founder, National Cash Register

Have not great merchants, great manufacturers, great inventors, done more for the world than preachers and philanthropists? ... Can there be any doubt that cheapening the cost of necessaries and conveniences of life is the most powerful agent of civilization and progress?

— CHARLES ELLIOTT PERKINS, 19th century railroad executive

I've got to keep breathing. It'll be my worst business mistake if I don't.

— SIR NATHAN ROTHSCHILD, financier and member of the British Parliament

We presumed that the first purpose in making a capital investment is the establishment of a business that will pay satisfactory dividends and preserve and increase its capital value. The primary object of the corporation, therefore, we declared, was to make money, not just motor cars.

— ALFRED P. SLOAN, JR., president and CEO, General Motors, 1923-1946

Passion. Creativity. Commitment. Those are the qualities that companies need most if they want to win in the new world of business. Those are also the qualities that are lacking at most companies.

— JIM STUART, cofounder, The Leadership Circle

The purpose of a business is to create a mutually beneficial relationship between itself and those that it serves. When it does that well, it will be around tomorrow to do it some more.

— JOHN WOODS, president, CWL Publishing Enterprises

Business occupies in the American scheme of things a place it occupies nowhere else in the world. The position of business in the American institutional framework is one of major significance.

> ━JAMES C. WORTHY, professor of management, J.L. Kellogg Graduate School of Management, Northwestern University, and author, *Shaping an American Institution: Robert E. Wood and Sears, Roebuck* (1984)

Capitalism

Capitalism without bankruptcy is like Christianity without hell.

> ━FRANK BORMAN, astronaut and business executive

A handful of capitalists has done infinitely more for mankind than all the self-serving politicians, academics, social workers, and religionists who march under the banner of "compassion."

> ━NATHANIEL BRANDEN, author, *The Art of Living Consciously*

Upon the sacredness of property civilization itself depends—the right of the laborer to his hundred dollars in the savings bank, and equally the legal right of the millionaire to his millions.

> ━ANDREW CARNEGIE, founder, U.S. Steel

Some regard private enterprise as if it were a predatory tiger to be shot. Others look upon it as a cow that they can milk. Only a handful see it for what it really is—the strong horse that pulls the whole cart.

> ━WINSTON CHURCHILL, former Prime Minister, Great Britain

I'd say capitalism's worst excess is in the large number of crooks and tinhorns who get too much of the action.

> ━MALCOLM FORBES, former publisher, *Forbes* magazine

The highest use of capital is not to make more money, but to make money do more for the betterment of life.
— HENRY FORD, founder, Ford Motor Company

I sometimes suspect that many American capitalists actually distrust the market as much as capitalism's enemies do.... There are whole industries today that prefer to escape the market's discipline.
— HENRY FORD, II, grandson of Henry Ford and former chairman, Ford Motor Company

History suggests that capitalism is a necessary condition for political freedom. Clearly it is not a sufficient condition.
— MILTON FRIEDMAN, economist

Under capitalism, man exploits man. Under communism, it's just the opposite.
— JOHN KENNETH GALBRAITH, economist

Doing well is the result of doing good. That's what capitalism is all about.
— ADNAN KASHOGGI, Saudi Arabian arms merchant and billionaire

When the operations of capitalism come to resemble those of the casino, ill fortune will be the lot of the many.
— JOHN MAYNARD KEYNES, economist

Capitalists are almost as much interested as laborers, in placing the operations of industry on such a footing that those who labor for them may feel the same interest in the work which is felt by those who labor on their own account.
— JOHN STUART MILL, economist

The forces of a capitalistic society, if left unchecked, tend to make the rich richer and the poor poorer.
— JAWAHARLAL NEHRU, first Prime Minister, India

Markets are said to possess wisdom that is somehow superior to man. Those of us in business who travel in the developing world see the results of such western wisdom and have a rumbling disquiet about much of what our economic institutions have bought into.

— ANITA RODDICK, founder, The Body Shop

Capitalism inevitably and by virtue of the very logic of its civilization creates, educates, and subsidizes a vested interest in social unrest.

— JOSEPH A. SCHUMPETER, economist

Career Development

Times have changed. Really changed. There is no such thing as "a career" as we have known it in the past. You can no longer depend on a steady job with regular promotions at the same company over a prolonged period. The conveyor belt that once hauled employees forward and upward has jerked to a halt, and the floor is littered with casualties.

— PAT ALEA AND PATTY MULLINS, authors, *The Best Work of Your Life*

[Humanities graduates] achieved the best overall performance, and were most suited for change, which is the leading future of the high-speed, high-tech world we now occupy.

— CHARLES L. BROWN, former chairman and CEO, AT&T

You cannot push anyone up the ladder unless he is willing to climb himself.

— ANDREW CARNEGIE, founder, U.S. Steel

In order to be irreplaceable one must always be different.

— COCO CHANEL, fashion designer

Self-marketing requires the basic textbook approach, including recognition of the need, target marketing, positioning, pricing, and development of a communications strategy.

➤ J. PAUL COSTELLO, cofounder, Costello, Erdlen and Co., cofounder of Restrac (now Webhire), and founder, Corporate Staffing Center, Inc.

All things being equal, the career person who is going to get ahead is not going to get ahead because he does great work. That is a given. We expect that. What will get him ahead is the edge he creates.

➤ JEFFREY P. DAVIDSON, management and marketing consultant and author

Beware of a misfit occupation…. Consider carefully your natural bent, whether for business or a profession.

➤ MARSHALL FIELD, founder, Marshall Field Department Stores

When those with ability at their job get to thinking they can't be done without, they're already on their way out.

➤ MALCOLM FORBES, former publisher, *Forbes* magazine

Advancement often depends not on rightness of action, but on acceptable behavior and image, e.g., self-control, appearance and dress, perception as a team player, style and patron power. The result of all this is ethical erosion.

➤ ROBERT W. GODDARD, publications director, Liberty Mutual Insurance

A résumé is a balance sheet without any liabilities.

➤ ROBERT HALF, founder, Robert Half International

Job mobility is connected to job competence, and vice versa.

➤ HAROLD S. HOOK, CEO, American General Corporation

You are your first product, so positioning yourself in the market as an individual is extremely important.

➤ PORTIA ISAACSON, president, Dream IT, Inc.

We are CEOs of our own companies: Me Inc. To be in business today, our most important job is to be head marketer for the brand called You.

— TOM PETERS, author and consultant

Challenge

It is good to be without vices, but it is not good to be without temptations.

— WALTER BAGEHOT, founding editor, *The Economist*

Kites rise highest against the wind—not with it.

— WINSTON CHURCHILL, former Prime Minister, Great Britain

If you're going through hell, keep going.

— WINSTON CHURCHILL

The mere fact that you have obstacles to overcome is in your favor.

— ROBERT COLLIER, master copywriter and author, *The Secret of the Ages*

A man of character finds a special attractiveness in difficulty, since it is only by coming to grips with difficulty that he can realize his potentialities.

— CHARLES DE GAULLE, former President, France

You may not realize it when it happens, but a kick in the teeth may be the best thing in the world for you.

— WALT DISNEY, founder, The Walt Disney Company

If you have a job without any aggravations, you don't have a job.

— MALCOLM FORBES, former publisher, *Forbes* magazine

When someone offers you a challenge, don't think of all the reasons why you can't do it. Instead, say, "Yes!" Then figure out how
you'll get it done.
> ━KATHERINE HUDSON, president and CEO, W. H. Brady Co.

If at times our actions seem to have made life difficult for others, it
is only because history has made life difficult for us all.
> ━JOHN F. KENNEDY, U.S. President

Problems are the price of progress. Don't bring me anything but
trouble—good news weakens me.
> ━CHARLES F. KETTERING, president, General Motors Research Corp.
> and cofounder, Sloan-Kettering Institute for Cancer Research

The ultimate measure of a man is not where he stands in moments
of comfort, but where he stands at times of challenge and contro-
versy.
> ━MARTIN LUTHER KING, JR., American civil rights leader

You must constantly guard against the trap of falling into a routine
of remaining busy with unimportant chores that will provide you
with an excuse to avoid meaningful challenges or opportunities
that could change your life for the better.
> ━OG MANDINO, inspirational speaker and author of several books
> including *The Greatest Secret in the World*

The greatness comes not when things go always good for you. But
the greatness comes when you're really tested, when you take some
knocks, some disappointments, when sadness comes.
> ━RICHARD M. NIXON, U.S. President

I would never have amounted to anything were it not for adversity.
I was forced to come up the hard way.
> ━JAMES C. PENNEY, founder, J.C. Penney stores

Life's challenges are not supposed to paralyze you, they're supposed to help you discover who you are.

— BERNICE JOHNSON REAGON, **curator emeritus, Smithsonian Institute**

The hardest struggle of all is to be something different from what the average man is.

— CHARLES M. SCHWAB, **former CEO, Bethlehem Steel**

There is more similarity in the marketing challenge of selling a precious painting by Degas and a frosted mug of root beer than you ever thought possible.

— ARTHUR TAUBMAN, **founder, Advance Auto Parts**

The response to the challenges of life—purpose—is the healing balm that enables each of us to face up to adversity and strife.

— DENIS WAITLEY, **author and consultant on "the psychology of winning"**

Change

All great changes are irksome to the human mind, especially those which are attended with great dangers and uncertain effects.

— JOHN QUINCY ADAMS, **U.S. President**

We're trying to change the habits of an awful lot of people. That won't happen overnight, but it bloody well will happen.

— JOHN AKERS, **former CEO, IBM**

Reorganization is the permanent condition of a vigorous organization.

— ROY ASH, **CEO, AM International**

Only in the frictionless vacuum of a nonexistent abstract world can movement or change occur without that abrasive friction of conflict.
— SAUL ALINSKY, U.S. political activist

In life, change is inevitable. In business, change is vital.
— WARREN BENNIS, founder and chair, Leadership Institute, University of Southern California

Those who have changed the universe have never done it by changing officials, but always by inspiring the people.
— NAPOLEON BONAPARTE, former emperor of France

A state without the means of some change is without the means of its conservation.
— EDMUND BURKE, former British statesman

There is no such thing as a permanent advertising success.
— LEO BURNETT, founder, Leo Burnett Advertising

The most important thing about change management, particularly for managers, is to recognize that you may not even know the truth about what is possible, that your whole cognition has been shaped by an experience in an industry that may no longer be relevant to the future.
— JAMES CHAMPY, chairman, Perot Systems Consulting

To improve is to change; to be perfect is to change often.
— WINSTON CHURCHILL, former Prime Minister, Great Britain

If we keep doing what we're doing, we're going to keep getting what we're getting.
— STEPHEN COVEY, consultant and author, *The 7 Habits of Highly Effective People*

If anything is certain, it is that change is certain. The world we are planning for today will not exist in this form tomorrow.
— PHILIP CROSBY, consultant and author, *Quality Is Free*

There will be times when people aren't able to react as quickly as technology changes. Managers ... must retrain their work forces for rapid evolution and flexibility. You don't want to shake them up for the sake of shaking them up, but you want to ... precondition the organization for change.

→ MICHAEL S. DELL, founder and chairman, Dell Computer

We cannot become what we want to be by remaining what we are.

→ MAX DEPREE, author, *Leadership Jazz,* and former CEO, Herman Miller, Inc.

Every organization has to prepare for the abandonment of everything it does.

→ PETER F. DRUCKER, consultant and renowned management author

People tend to overestimate the change that will occur in the next two years but underestimate the changes that will occur in the next ten.

→ BILL GATES, cofounder and chairman, Microsoft

There is danger in reckless change, but greater danger in blind conservatism.

→ HENRY GEORGE, economist and author, *Progress and Plenty*

Change can come with breathtaking speed, leaving a company on the defensive and in financial trouble when it's forced to catch up.

→ GARY GOLDSTICK AND GEORGE SCHREIBER, principals of Goldstick and Schreiber (now G.H. Goldstick & Co.)

Not all organizations adapt equally well to the environment within which they grow. Many, like the dinosaur of great size but little brain, remain unchanged in a changing world.

→ CHARLES HANDY, cofounder, London Business School, and author, *Understanding Organizations* and *Beyond Certainty: The Changing Worlds of Organizations*

All organizations do change when put under sufficient pressure. This pressure must be either external to the organization or the result of a very strong leadership.

→ BRUCE HENDERSON, former CEO, Boston Consulting Group

The world hates changes, yet it is the only thing that has brought progress.

→ CHARLES F. KETTERING, president, General Motors Research Corp., and cofounder, Sloan-Kettering Institute for Cancer Research

Today's peacock is tomorrow's feather duster.

→ ARTHUR MARTINEZ, CEO, Sears

The only [management] practice that's now constant is the practice of constantly accommodating to change.

→ WILLIAM G. MCGOWAN, founder, MCI Communications

The first step towards getting somewhere is to decide that you are not going to stay where you are.

→ J. PIERPONT MORGAN, American financier

The reason successful small companies learn to change is that, for their leaders, the locus of change is not in their heads but in their hearts.

→ IAN MORRISON, author, *The Second Curve: Managing the Velocity of Change*

There are only two ways to get people to support corporate change. You should give employees the information they need to understand the reasons for change, and put enough influence behind the information to [gain their] support.

→ CARLA O'DELL, president, American Productivity & Quality Center

Today, loving change, tumult, even chaos is a prerequisite for survival, let alone success.

— TOM PETERS, **author and consultant**

Success breeds conservatism, and that means a love affair with the status quo and an aversion to change.

— FRANK POPOFF, **CEO, Dow Chemical**

Employees don't resist change, they resist being changed.

— PETER SCHOLTES, **consultant and author,** *The Leader's Handbook*

Change requires knowledge. Improvement requires wisdom.

— PETER SCHOLTES

I always loved change, something new. Change is a challenge, an excitement.

— DAWN SIBLEY, **vice president, corporate media director, Western International Media**

Smart organizations of the future won't try to manage change processes. Instead they will nurture the spirit of change within their people. That way, change will occur naturally, and it will preserve the heart and soul of the organization.

— SUE SIMMONS, **vice president, Transition Concepts, Ltd.**

So much has been written about employees' resistance to change that we are sometimes tempted to forget that they can also react favorably.

— NATHANIEL STEWART, **director, Management Development Center, U.S. A.I.D.**

A competitive world has two possibilities for you. You can lose. Or, if you want to win, you can change.

— LESTER THUROW, **former dean, MIT Sloan School of Management**

Markets change, tastes change, so the companies and the individuals who choose to compete in those markets must change.

➤ AN WANG, founder, Wang Labs

Habit breaking, the prerequisite for change and renewal, needs more than a simple decision. It takes motivation, desire, and will. Crisis can provide that and all too often is the sole force for change.

➤ ROBERT H. WATERMAN, consultant and co-author, *In Search of Excellence*

I am convinced that if the rate of change inside an organization is less than the rate of change outside, the end is in sight.

➤ JACK WELCH, chairman and CEO, General Electric

Character

For years, I've seen women trying to act like men. More recently, I've seen men trying to act like women. It won't work. The only way to be powerfully successful, whether you're a man or a woman, is to be who you are.

➤ JESSICA BIBLIOWICZ, president and COO, John A. Levin

Be more concerned with your character than with your reputation. Your character is what you really are while your reputation is merely what others think you are.

➤ DALE CARNEGIE, author, *How to Win Friends and Influence People*

The character ethic, which I believe to be the foundation of success, teaches that there are basic principles of effective living, and that people can only experience true success and enduring happiness as they learn and integrate these principles into their basic character.

➤ STEPHEN COVEY, consultant and author, *The 7 Habits of Highly Effective People*

You can easily judge the character of others by how they treat those who can do nothing for them or to them.

— MALCOLM FORBES, former publisher, *Forbes* magazine

What lies ahead of you and what lies behind you is nothing compared to what lies within you.

— MOHANDAS K. GANDHI, leader, Indian independence movement

How you react when the joke's on you can reveal your character.

— ROBERT HALF, founder, Robert Half International

Many a man's reputation would not know his character if they met on the street.

— ELBERT HUBBARD, writer, editor, and founder, Roycroft Press

We define ourselves by the best that is in us, not the worst that has been done to us.

— EDWARD LEWIS, publisher, *Essence* magazine

Nearly all men can stand adversity, but if you want to test a man's character, give him power.

— ABRAHAM LINCOLN, U.S. President

The success or failure of the business doesn't necessarily have to do only with the numbers, but rather with the personalities and character of the people who run it. People get so impressed with what they have accomplished that they can no longer see themselves in the context of reality.

— DARLA MOORE, CEO, Rainwater Inc.

You can tell a lot about a fellow's character by the way he eats jelly beans.

— RONALD REAGAN, U.S. President

Bear in mind that brains and learning, like muscle and physical skill, are articles of commerce. They are bought and sold. You can hire them by the year or by the hour. The only thing in the world *not* for sale is character.

➥ANTONIN SCALIA, Associate Justice, U.S. Supreme Court

Leadership is a potent combination of strategy and character. But if you must be without one, be without the strategy.

➥H. NORMAN SCHWARZKOPF, general, commander, Gulf War

To feel much for others and little for ourselves, to restrain our selfishness and exercise our benevolent affections, constitute the perfection of human nature.

➥ADAM SMITH, economist

Really big people are, above everything else, courteous, considerate, and generous—not just to some people in some circumstances—but to everyone all the time.

➥THOMAS J. WATSON, JR., son of founder and former chairman, IBM

Character is doing what's right when nobody's looking.

➥J.C. WATTS, Congressional Representative, Oklahoma

Ability may get you to the top, but it takes character to keep you there.

➥JOHN WOODEN, former basketball coach, UCLA

⤳ *Commitment* ⤳

Whatever you do, do it with all your might. Work at it, early and late, in season and out of season, not leaving a stone unturned, and never deferring for a single hour that which can be done just as well as now.

— P. T. BARNUM, circus owner

Here is the prime condition of success: Having begun on one line, resolve to fight it out on that line, to lead in it, adopt every improvement, have the best machinery, and know the most about it.

— ANDREW CARNEGIE, founder, U. S. Steel

If you are committed to creating value, and if you aren't afraid of the hard times, obstacles become utterly unimportant.

— CANDICE CARPENTER, CEO, ivillage

[On commitment]: We're talking the heavy, deep, man/woman on a mission stuff. When the grenades are flying the committed person doesn't go AWOL. There is nothing more powerful than emotional equity. No amount of stock options even comes close.

— CHRISTINE COMAFORD, founder, Artemis Ventures

Unless commitment is made, there are only promises and hopes; but no plans.

— PETER F. DRUCKER, consultant and renowned management author

I remember committing myself to make it in the garbage business, "whatever it takes!"

— TOM FATJO, founder, Browning-Ferris Industries

Presence is more than just being there.

— MALCOLM FORBES, former publisher, *Forbes* magazine

A promise is an IOU.

    —ROBERT HALF, founder, Robert Half International

If you want to make good use of your time, you've got to know what's most important and then give it all you've got.

    —LEE IACOCCA, former chairman, Chrysler Corp.

The quality of a person's life is in direct proportion to their commitment to excellence, regardless of their chosen field of endeavor.

    —VINCE LOMBARDI, legendary coach, Green Bay Packers

Do your damnedest in an ostentatious manner all the time.

    —GEORGE S. PATTON, World War II general

Unless you are willing to drench yourself in your work beyond the capacity of the average person, you are just not cut out for positions at the top.

    —JAMES C. PENNEY, founder, J.C. Penney stores

The committed person doesn't play by "the rules of the game." He is responsible for the game. If the rules of the game stand in the way of achieving the vision, he will find ways to change the rules.

    —PETER SENGE, business professor and author, *The Fifth Discipline*

I found that the men and women who got to the top were those who did the jobs they had in hand, with everything they had of energy and enthusiasm and hard work.

    —HARRY S. TRUMAN, U.S. President

Commit to your business. Believe in it more than anything else. If you love your work, you'll be out there every day trying to do the best you can, and pretty soon everybody around will catch the passion from you.

    —SAM WALTON, founder, Wal-Mart

You have to have your heart in the business and the business in your heart.

    —THOMAS J. WATSON, SR., founder, IBM

Communication

[To improve communications practices of computer departments] … you have to break the back of the bureaucracy you've established.

    —MICHAEL ALBRECHT, JR., principal, Nolan, Norton

[The] first function of the executive is to develop and maintain a system of communication.

    —CHESTER I. BARNARD, author, *The Functions of the Executive* (1938)

The ability to express an idea is well nigh as important as the idea itself.

    —BERNARD BARUCH, American financier and presidential advisor

In communications, familiarity breeds apathy.

    —WILLIAM BERNBACH, cofounder, DDB Needham Advertising

When you have nothing important or interesting to say, don't let anyone persuade you to say it.

    —H. JACKSON BROWN, JR., author, *Life's Little Instruction Book*

If you want to change your company, radically increase the span of communication for each individual. Let each person use a computer to communicate with anybody in the company—or anywhere else in the world—without any barriers, real or imagined.

    —ROBERT H. BUCKMAN, vice chairman, Buckman Laboratories International

This report, by its very length, defends itself against the risk of being read.

— WINSTON CHURCHILL, former Prime Minister, Great Britain

The very best financial presentation is one that's well thought out and anticipates any questions … answering them in advance.

— NATHAN COLLINS, executive VP, Valley National Bank

The good time-users among managers … do not talk to their subordinates about their problems, but they know how to make the subordinates talk about theirs.

— PETER F. DRUCKER, consultant and renowned management author

Ninety percent of leadership is the ability to communicate something people want.

— DIANE FEINSTEIN, U.S. Senator, California

We all want to be judged by how good we are when we're at our creative best. But the real test is how good we are when we're at our creative average.

— BILL FLANAGAN, vice president of programming and editorial director, VH1

If you say what you think, don't expect to hear only what you like.

— MALCOLM FORBES, former publisher, *Forbes* magazine

The most important element in establishing a happy, prosperous atmosphere was an insistence upon open, free, and honest communications up and down the ranks of our management structure.

— HAROLD GENEEN, former CEO, IT&T

Communicate unto the other guy that which you would want him to communicate unto you if your positions were reversed.

— AARON GOLDMAN, CEO, The Macke Company

The worse the news, the more effort should go into communicating it.
  ━ANDREW S. GROVE, former CEO, Intel Corp.

How well we communicate is determined not by how well we say things but by how well we are understood.
  ━ANDREW S. GROVE

Silence is argument carried on by other means.
  ━CHE GUEVARA, theoretician and tactician of guerrilla warfare

The right to be heard does not automatically include the right to be taken seriously. To be taken seriously depends entirely upon what is being said.
  ━HUBERT H. HUMPHREY, senator and presidential candidate

Storytelling will ... affect the way companies hire and retain employees. Companies will recruit people based on how they express their spirit. Marx may have been right: In an ideal society, employees will own the means of production—in their heads and in their hearts.
  ━ROLF JENSEN, director, The Copenhagen Institute for Futures Studies, and author, *The Dream Society*

There is no quicker way for two executives to get out of touch with each other than to retire to the seclusion of their offices and write each other notes.
  ━R. ALEC MACKENZIE, management consultant and author, *The Time Trap* (1972)

Communication is not just words, paint on canvas, math symbols or the equations and models of scientists; it is the interrelation of human beings trying to escape loneliness, trying to share experience, trying to implant ideas.
  ━WILLIAM M. MARSTELLER, cofounder, Burson-Marsteller public relations agency and author, *Creative Management*

What is it about ... organizations that make certain kinds of truth and certain kinds of expression not suitable or appropriate?
— ABRAHAM MASLOW, psychologist and author, *Maslow on Management*

It is ironic, but true, that in this age of electronic communications, personal interaction is becoming more important than ever.
— REGIS McKENNA, chairman, The McKenna Group

People act and respond more openly in a phone meeting than they would in memos or one-on-one meetings with their boss.
— RON OWENS, VP, Houghton Mifflin

If an organization is to work effectively, the communication should be through the most effective channel regardless of the organization chart.
— DAVID PACKARD, cofounder, Hewlett-Packard

Written reports stifle creativity.
— H. ROSS PEROT, founder, EDS and Perot Systems

Communication is everyone's panacea for everything.
— TOM PETERS, author and consultant

People, including managers, do not live by pie charts alone—or by bar graphs or three-inch statistical appendices to 300-page reports. People live, reason, and are moved by symbols and stories.
— TOM PETERS

The exact words that you use are far less important than the energy, intensity, and conviction with which you use them.
— JULES ROSE, VP, Sloan Supermarkets

Hurried speech is a form of deference.
— EARL SHORRIS, contributing editor, *Harper's* magazine

Communicate everything you possibly can to your partners. The more they understand, the more they'll care. Once they care, there's no stopping them.

—SAM WALTON, founder, Wal-Mart

You can't *not* communicate. Everything you say and do or don't say and don't do sends a message to others.

—JOHN WOODS, president, CWL Publishing Enterprises

Our words do not describe things but our relationship to things. In this lies the heart of misunderstanding.

—JOHN WOODS

Am I an elementary school student? Why do you insist on writing wordy reports and giving presentations for hours on issues that could be solved through a phone call or an e-mail message?

—YUN JONG YONG, CEO, Samsung Electronics

Competence

Competent [people] in every position, if they are doing their best, know all that there is to know about their work except how to improve it.

—W. EDWARDS DEMING, consultant and author, *Out of the Crisis*

To blame a promotion that fails on the promoted person, as is usually done, is no more rational than to blame a capital investment that has gone sour on the money that was put into it.

—PETER F. DRUCKER, consultant and renowned management author

You have deep engineering prowess. I bring strategic vision, which HP needs.

➤ CARLY FIORINA, chairman and CEO, Hewlett-Packard

Looking the part helps get the chance to fill it. But if you fill the part, it matters not if you look it.

➤ MALCOLM FORBES, former publisher, *Forbes* magazine

Competent people have a predictable, reliable process for solving a particular set of problems. They solve a problem the same way, every time. That's what makes them reliable. That's what makes them competent.

➤ SETH GODIN, founder and president, Yoyodyne Entertainment, and vice president, direct marketing, Yahoo!

I'm a manager and I'm a teacher and I understand banking, and for that reason I am president of this bank.

➤ ROSEMARIE GRECO, former president, CoreStates Financial, and principal, GRECOventures

I don't have time to distinguish between the unfortunate and the incompetent.

➤ CURTIS LE MAY, World War II general, and former Chief of Staff, U.S. Air Force

The most important wings on an airplane are on the pilot.

➤ T. ALLEN MCARTOR, administrator, FAA

The single most exciting thing you encounter in government is competence, because it's so rare.

➤ DANIEL PATRICK MOYNIHAN, U.S. Senator, New York

Competition

We were fairly arrogant, until we realized the Japanese were selling quality products for what it cost us to make them.
— PAUL A. ALLAIRE, chairman, Xerox Corp.

The cosmetics industry is the nastiest business in the world.
— ELIZABETH ARDEN, founder, Elizabeth Arden Cosmetics

You don't have to blow out the other fellow's light to let your own shine.
— BERNARD BARUCH, American financier and presidential advisor

The company with the second best organization ends up second place in the market.
— D. WAYNE CALLOWAY, former chairman, Pepsico

I have to convince the 160,000 people who work for Peugeot about how terrifying the competition is.... We will just have to be a little faster.
— JACQUES CALVERT, former chairman, Peugeot

The first man gets the oyster, the second man gets the shell.
— ANDREW CARNEGIE, founder, U.S. Steel

It turns out that you can actually prosper more by entering into relationships of reciprocation, so that you're both getting more than either of you would have gotten separately.
— HELENA CRONIN, codirector, Centre for Philosophy of Natural and Social Science, London School of Economics

The most important thing in the Olympic Games is not winning but taking part .... The essential thing in life is not conquering but fighting well.
— PIERRE DE COUBERTIN, former president, International Olympic Committee

The competitor to be feared is one who never bothers about you at all, but goes on making his own business better all the time.

—HENRY FORD, founder, Ford Motor Company

Competition whose motive is merely to compete, to drive some other fellow out, never carries very far.

—HENRY FORD

[America's] competitors have learned how to do what we invented *better* and *faster* than we do.

—STANLEY C. GAULT, former CEO, Rubbermaid and Goodyear Tire & Rubber

I don't look back because they might be gaining on us. Besides, there's always going to be competition.

—EARL G. GRAVES, publisher, *Black Enterprise*

Concentrate your strength against your competitor's relative weakness.

—BRUCE HENDERSON, former CEO, Boston Consulting Group

In business, the competition will bite you if you keep running; if you stand still, they will swallow you.

—WILLIAM S. KNUDSEN, former president, General Motors

It is ridiculous to call this an industry. This is rat eat rat, dog eat dog. I'll kill 'em, and I'm going to kill 'em before they kill me. You're talking about the American way of survival of the fittest.

—RAY KROC, founder, McDonald's

There is no room for second place. There is only one place in my game and that is first place. I have finished second twice in my time at Green Bay and I never want to finish second again.

—VINCE LOMBARDI, legendary coach, Green Bay Packers

When you lose get mad—but get mad at yourself, not your opponent.

— WALLACE "CHIEF" NEWMAN, **former football coach, Whittier College (quoted by Richard Nixon)**

Although we feel very strongly about competitive spirit, we feel it should be vented against our real competition outside, not within the company.

— FRANCIS P. RICH, JR., **president, Action Equipment Co.**

Next to knowing all about your own business, the best thing is to know all about the other fellow's business.

— JOHN D. ROCKEFELLER, **founder, Standard Oil**

The thrill, believe me, is as much in the battle as in the victory.

— DAVID SARNOFF, **founder, RCA**

Competition brings out the best in products and the worst in people.

— ROBERT W. SARNOFF, **son of David Sarnoff and head of NBC**

The minute you start talking about what you're going to do if you lose, you have lost.

— GEORGE SCHULTZ, **former Secretary of State, Reagan Administration and executive, Bechtel Corporation**

Don't limit your definition of the competition. Think outside the box! The conventional boundaries that separate industries mean less and less; develop your peripheral vision to scope out latent competitors.

— MIKE SLADE, **CEO, Starwave Corp.**

Treating a competitor's brand as if it didn't exist doesn't mean your customers will do the same.

— MARGIE SMITH, **Sr. VP, Mark Ponton Co.**

If I'm doing business with Marriott, I'd better be able to service Marriott all over the country. If I can't, somebody else is going to come in who can.

—SANDY SOLOMON, founder, Sweet Streets Desserts, Inc.

Compromise

You can be very bold as a theoretician. Good theories are like good art. A practitioner has to compromise.

—WARREN BENNIS, founder and chair, Leadership Institute, University of Southern California

The effective executive knows that to get strength one has to put up with weaknesses.

—PETER F. DRUCKER, consultant and renowned management author

If you never budge, don't expect a push.

—MALCOLM FORBES, former publisher, *Forbes* magazine

Adaptability is not imitation. It means power of resistance and assimilation.

—MOHANDAS K. GANDHI, leader, Indian independence movement

Strong men don't compromise, it is said, and principles should never be compromised. I shall argue that strong men, conversely, know when to compromise and that all principles can be compromised to serve a greater principle.

—CHARLES HANDY, cofounder, London Business School, and author, *Understanding Organizations* and *Beyond Certainty: The Changing Worlds of Organizations*

A man who trims himself to suit everybody will soon whittle himself away.

—Charles M. Schwab, former CEO, Bethlehem Steel

Compromise is usually bad. It should be a last resort. If two departments or divisions have a problem they can't solve and it comes up to you, listen to both sides and then … pick one or the other. This places solid accountability on the winner to make it work. Condition your people to avoid compromise.

—Robert Townsend, former CEO, Avis Rent-a-Car, and author, *Up the Organization*

Computers

One of the most feared expressions in modern times is "The computer is down."

—Norman Augustine, president and CEO, Lockheed Martin

Instead of viewing the PC as a productivity machine, we've turned it into a communication device. It about … building a sense of community and engaging people.

—Steve Case, founder and CEO, America Online

I think the phrase "computer-literate" is an evil phrase. You don't have to be "automobile-literate" to get along in this world. You don't have to be "telephone-literate." Why should you have to be "computer-literate"?

—Alan Cooper, principal, Cooper Interactive Design

The main impact of the computer has been the provision of unlimited jobs for clerks.

➤PETER F. DRUCKER, **consultant and renowned management author**

The computer is merely a tool in the process.... To put it in editorial terms, knowing how a typewriter works does not make you a writer. Now that knowledge is taking the place of capital as the driving force in organizations worldwide, it is all too easy to confuse data with knowledge and information technology with information.

➤PETER F. DRUCKER

A computer will not make a good manager out of a bad manager. It makes a good manager better faster and a bad manager worse faster.

➤EDWARD M. ESBER, **former CEO, Ashton-Tate**

I really don't care that I don't have what's current because whatever is at the moment, it will be infinitely better in a few months and even better months later.

➤WILLIAM FINK, **superintendent, National Park Service**

Anyone who spends their life on a computer is pretty unusual.

➤BILL GATES, **cofounder and chairman, Microsoft**

We'll get machines that are a million times faster over the next 10 years. ... The key message here is that we are just at the beginning of the revolution—today's machines are Model T's.

➤BILL GATES (1998)

There is an absolute correlation between U.S. industry's investments in information technology and the ever-lengthening cycle of American economic growth. Perhaps the most profound impact of these investments will be with smaller businesses, which we all know are the greatest source of job creation and economic expansion in America today.

➤LOU GERSTNER, **chairman and CEO, IBM**

Computers can automate the mechanics of work of all kinds—whether they generate payroll checks or perform sophisticated statistical analyses. So far they cannot even come close to doing the kind of work that involves *judgment* on the part of managers.

　→ANDREW S. GROVE, **former CEO, Intel Corp.**

We can remove the constraints of distance and time by using the electronic networking of people. ... You can't "beam me up," but you can be there electronically.

　→DAVE HOUSE, **chairman, CEO, and president, Bay Networks Inc.**

The personal computer is a tool that can amplify a certain part of our inherent intelligence.

　→STEVEN JOBS, **cofounder and CEO, Apple Computer**

This is what customers pay us for—to sweat all the details so it's easy and pleasant for them to use our computers.

　→STEVEN JOBS

Training is probably the most important aspect of buying a computer system.

　→BARRY KNOWLES, **owner, Valcom Computer Center**

"Our computer's down." This is another great [business] lie. Unfortunately, it is true so often that you seldom can attack it head on.

　→CHARLES W. KYD, **president, IncSight Corporation**

The value of any network increases in proportion to the square of the number of people using it, so a network with five hundred people attached to it is a hundred times as useful as one with only fifty people attached.

　→ROBERT METCALFE, **inventor of Ethernet, founder, 3COM, and vice president of technology, International Data Group**

The technology of the computer allows us to have a distinct individually tailored arrangement with each of thousands of employees.

　→JOHN NAISBITT, **former executive, IBM and Eastman Kodak, author of *Megatrends*, *Global Paradox*, and *High Tech/High Touch***

We created the hierarchical, pyramidal, managerial system because we needed to keep track of people and the things people did; with the computer to keep track, we can restructure our institutions horizontally.
——JOHN NAISBITT, former executive, IBM and Eastman Kodak, author of *Megatrends*, *Global Paradox*, and *High Tech/High Touch*

Machines should work. People should think.
——JOHN PEERS, president, Logical Machine Corporation

Always remember what you originally wanted the system to accomplish. Having the latest, greatest system and a flashy data center to boot is not what data processing is supposed to be all about. It is supposed to help the bottom line, not hinder it.
——RICHARD S. RUBIN, telecommunications manager, Citibank

Confidence

Aerodynamically the bumble bee shouldn't be able to fly, but the bumble bee doesn't know it, so it goes on flying anyway.
——MARY KAY ASH, founder, Mary Kay Cosmetics

If you think you can, you can. And if you think you can't, you're right.
——MARY KAY ASH

The word impossible is not in my dictionary.
——NAPOLEON BONAPARTE, former emperor of France

Immense power is acquired by assuring yourself in your secret reveries that you were born to control affairs.
——ANDREW CARNEGIE, founder, U.S. Steel

Naturalness is the easiest thing in the world to acquire, if you will forget yourself, forget about the impression you are trying to make.

> ━DALE CARNEGIE, author, *How to Win Friends and Influence People*

Business places no premiums on shrinking violets. Employers prefer men who have self-assurance, forcefulness, go-aheadness, men who know their jobs and know that they know it.

> ━B.C. FORBES, founder, *Forbes* magazine

The ultimate high: A man's abilities equaling his opinion of 'em.

> ━MALCOLM FORBES, former publisher, *Forbes* magazine

When you have confidence, you can have a lot of fun. And when you have fun, you can do amazing things.

> ━JOE NAMATH, former NFL player and business person

Besides pride, loyalty, discipline, heart, and mind, confidence is the key to all the locks.

> ━JOE PATERNO, football coach, Penn State University

No one can make you feel small without your consent.

> ━ELEANOR ROOSEVELT, former First Lady

Whenever you are asked if you can do a job, tell 'em, "Certainly, I can!" Then get busy and find out how to do it.

> ━THEODORE ROOSEVELT, U.S. President

It is courage based on confidence, not daring, and it is confidence based on experience.

> ━JONAS SALK, developer, polio vaccine and founder, Salk Institute

If you're going to take gambles, you must have one thing: self-confidence.

> ━DON SHULA, former coach, Miami Dolphins

Self-confident people are open to good ideas regardless of their source and are willing to share them. Their egos don't require that they originate every idea they use or get credit for every idea they originate.
—JACK WELCH, chairman and CEO, General Electric

The world is exactly like we think it is, and that's why.
—JOHN WOODS, president, CWL Publishing Enterprises

Conflict

I'm not one to waste energy and time having arguments.
—RICHARD BRANSON, founder, Virgin Group

The only way to get the best of an argument is to avoid it.
—DALE CARNEGIE, author, *How to Win Friends and Influence People*

Difficulties are meant to rouse, not discourage. The human spirit is to grow strong by conflict.
—WILLIAM ELLERY CHANNING, 19th-century minister, abolitionist, and essayist

Parliament can compel people to obey or to submit, but it cannot compel them to agree.
—WINSTON CHURCHILL, former Prime Minister, Great Britain

The competent executive is able to consider many points of view.... An executive's life consists of reconciling points of view that often seem, and sometimes are irreconcilable.
—ABRAM T. COLLIER, CEO, New England Mutual

Where you want the contest is not among people, but among ideas.
—CASEY COWELL, cofounder, U.S. Robotics, and chairman and principal owner, Durandal, Inc., a holding company

Why is there no conflict at this meeting? Something's wrong when there's no conflict.

— Michael Eisner, chairman and CEO, The Walt Disney Company

An association of men who will not quarrel with one another is a thing which never yet existed, from the greatest confederacy of nations down to a town meeting or a vestry.

— Thomas Jefferson, U.S. President

We will have differences. ... Even in our own country we do not see everything alike. If we did, we would all want the same wife— and that would be a problem, wouldn't it?

— Lyndon B. Johnson, U.S. President

Instead of suppressing conflicts, specific channels could be created to make this conflict explicit, and specific methods could be set up by which the conflict is resolved.

— Albert Low, author, *Zen and Creative Management*

It is impossible to defeat an ignorant man in a argument.

— William Gibbs McAdoo, president, the New York and New Jersey Railroad Company and the Hudson and Manhattan Railroad, Secretary of the Treasury, and U.S. Senator

Our differences are policies, our agreements principles.

— William McKinley, U.S. President

Like everybody else, once in a while we have a desk pounding or two.

— James Ortega, partner, Best Western Paving Co.

Most executives are uneasy with conflict and things that seem contradictory. They seek the middle ground, and inevitably the result is mediocrity; organizations without distinction and lacking creative tension. Too little constructive disagreement lulls an organization into complacency.

— Richard Pascale, consultant, associate fellow of Templeton College, Oxford University, and author, *Managing on the Edge: How the Smartest Companies Use Conflict to Stay Ahead*

People need a chance to see how much agreement is possible between seemingly intractable opponents.
—ROBERT REDFORD, founder, Sundance Institute

A good manager doesn't try to eliminate conflict; he tries to keep it from wasting the energies of his people. If you're the boss and your people fight you openly when they think you are wrong—that's healthy.
—ROBERT TOWNSEND, former CEO, Avis Rent-a-Car, and author, *Up the Organization*

Intense feeling too often obscures the truth.
—HARRY S. TRUMAN, U.S. President

 *Conformity*

So long as there are earnest believers in the world, they will always wish to punish opinions, even if their judgment tells them it is unwise and their conscience that it is wrong.
—WALTER BAGEHOT, founding editor, *The Economist*

Choose your own direction—rather than climb on the bandwagon.
—PETER F. DRUCKER, consultant and renowned management author

In matters of conscience, the law of the majority has no place.
—MOHANDAS K. GANDHI, leader, Indian independence movement

No one can possibly achieve any real and lasting success or "get rich" in business by being a conformist.
—J. PAUL GETTY, founder, Getty Oil

To swallow and follow, whether old doctrine or new propaganda, is a weakness still dominating the human mind.

⟵CHARLOTTE PERKINS GILMAN, founder, *The Forerunner* (magazine), and author, *Women and Economics*

If birds of a feather flock together, they don't learn enough.

⟵ROBERT HALF, founder, Robert Half International

It's amazing what ordinary people can do if they set out without preconceived notions.

⟵CHARLES KETTERING, president, General Motors Research Corp., and cofounder, Sloan-Kettering Institute for Cancer Research

Where all men think alike, no one thinks very much.

⟵WALTER LIPPMANN, journalist and presidential advisor

How can great minds be produced in a country where the test of great minds is agreeing in the opinion of small minds?

⟵JOHN STUART MILL, economist

If you want to get along, go along.

⟵SAM RAYBURN, former Speaker of the House of Representatives

New ideas ... are not born in a conforming environment.

⟵ROGER VON OECH, consultant and author, *A Whack on the Side of the Head*

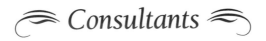

Consultants

All too many consultants, when asked, "What is 2 and 2?" respond, "What do you have in mind?"

⟵NORMAN AUGUSTINE, president and CEO, Lockheed Martin

The contribution I make to a client is basically to be very stupid and very dense; ask simple, fundamental questions; demand that he be thoughtful with the answers; and demand that he makes decisions on what is important.

— PETER F. DRUCKER, consultant and renowned management author

A consultant solves other people's problems. I could never do that. I want to help other people solve their own problems.

— CHARLES HANDY, cofounder, London Business School, and author, *Understanding Organizations* and *Beyond Certainty: The Changing Worlds of Organizations*

I don't like to hire consultants. They're like castrated bulls; all they can do is advise.

— VICTOR KIAM, CEO, Remington Products

I don't want a lawyer to tell me what I cannot do; I hire them to tell me how to do what I want to do.

— J. PIERPONT MORGAN, American fiancier

Consultants have strong professional values, a very strong sense of independence but they don't like being responsible for lots of people. Being a consultant is the next best thing to being self-employed.

— ARCHIE NORMAN, chair, ASDA Group plc (UK) supermarket chain, and Member of Parliament

Consultants are people who borrow your watch and tell you what time it is, and then walk off with the watch.

— ROBERT TOWNSEND, former CEO, Avis Rent-a-Car, and author, *Up the Organization*

I said that an expert was a fella who was afraid to learn anything new because then he wouldn't be an expert anymore.

— HARRY S. TRUMAN, U.S. President

 *Conviction*

There is no place in a fanatic's head where reason can enter.
— NAPOLEON BONAPARTE, **former emperor of France**

It is a fine thing to be honest, but it is very important for a Prime Minister to be right.
— WINSTON CHURCHILL, **former Prime Minister, Great Britain**

Duty cannot exist without faith.
— BENJAMIN DISRAELI, **19th century Prime Minister, Great Britain**

He who sees the truth, let him proclaim it, without asking who is for it or who is against it.
— HENRY GEORGE, **economist and author,** *Progress and Plenty*

The success or failure of any company boils down to one question: Are you operating from passion? If you are, you're going to succeed. If you believe in what you're doing, you're going to make sure that everyone around you believes in it too.
— MAGGIE HUGHES, **president and COO, LifeUSA Holding Inc.**

If you want to make good use of your time, you've got to know what's most important and then give it all you've got.
— LEE IACOCCA, **former chairman, Chrysler Corp.**

What convinces is conviction. Believe in the argument you are advancing. If you don't you're as good as dead.
— LYNDON B. JOHNSON, **U.S. President**

If both factions, or neither, shall abuse you, you will probably be about right. Beware of being assailed by one and praised by the other.
— ABRAHAM LINCOLN, **U.S. President**

One person with a belief is equal to a force of ninety-nine who have only interests.
　　—JOHN STUART MILL, economist

Good copy can't be written with tongue in cheek, written just for a living. You've got to believe in the product.
　　—DAVID OGILVY, cofounder, Ogilvy & Mather Advertising

I want something not just to invest in. I want something to believe in.
　　—ANITA RODDICK, founder, The Body Shop

The thing you really believe in always happens ... and the belief in a thing makes it happen.
　　—FRANK LLOYD WRIGHT, architect

Cooperation

Great discoveries and improvement invariably involve the cooperation of many minds. I may be given credit for having blazed the trail, but when I look at the subsequent developments I feel the credit is due to others rather than to myself.
　　—ALEXANDER GRAHAM BELL, inventor of the telephone

Ninety percent of the art the living consists of getting on with people one cannot stand.
　　—SAMUEL GOLDWYN, cofounder, Metro-Goldwyn-Mayer Studios

One uncooperative employee can sabotage an entire organization because bad spirit is more contagious than good spirit.
　　—ROBERT HALF, founder, Robert Half International

There is a point in all situation of conflict where both parties gain more or lose less from peace than they can hope to gain from any foreseeable victory. Beyond that point cooperation is more profitable than conflict.

→ BRUCE HENDERSON, CEO, Boston Consulting Group

Companies that cling to a "go it alone" mentality are in danger of going the way of the dinosaur as we move toward the 21st century.

→ LORENZO NECCI, president, EniChem

In unity there is strength. Consider the fragile snowflake that flutters slowly to earth and disintegrates; however, if enough of them stick together they can paralyze an entire city.

→ WILLIAM ROSENBERG, founder, Dunkin' Donuts

John Adams and Thomas Jefferson were political enemies, but they became fast friends. And when they passed away on the same day, the last words of one of them were, "The country is safe. Jefferson still lives." And the last words of the other were, "John Adams will see that things go forward."

→ HARRY S. TRUMAN, U.S. PRESIDENT

I've never been bashful about asking for help.

→ TED TURNER, CEO, Turner Broadcasting

We're all working together; that's the secret.

→ SAM WALTON, founder, Wal-Mart

Competition is just a particular form of cooperation.

→ JOHN WOODS, president, CWL Publishing Enterprises

Corporate Culture

Creative ideas flourish best in a shop that preserves some spirit of fun. Nobody is in business for fun, but that does not mean there cannot be fun in business.

— LEO BURNETT, founder, Leo Burnett Advertising

We must learn how to see the company as a living system and to see it as a system within the context of the larger systems of which it is a part. Only then will our vision reliably include return for our shareholders, a productive environment for our employees, and a social vision for the company as a whole.

— PHIL CARROLL, CEO, Shell Oil

The key participation question: "Would you rather work as part of an outstanding group, or be a part of a group of outstanding individuals?"

— MAX DEPREE, author, *Leadership Jazz* and former CEO, Herman Miller, Inc.

There is a lesson that lies in the foundation of my business—there is no such thing as an insignificant human being. To treat people that way is a kind of sin, and there's no reason for it, none.

— DEBBI FIELDS, founder, Mrs. Fields' Cookies

You've got to have an atmosphere where people can make mistakes. If we're not making mistakes we're not going anywhere.

— GORDON FORWARD, president, Chaparral Steel

Companies need to be able to outlive their leaders. One of the great examples of this is the HP Way: People who come to work at Hewlett-Packard know what the HP Way is.

— MARY FURLONG, founder, ThirdAge Media

Every company has two organizational structures: The formal one is written on the charts; the other is the everyday relationship of the men and women of the organization
    ← HAROLD GENEEN, former CEO, IT&T

A strong corporate culture is the invisible hand that guides how things are done in an organization. The phrase, "You just can't do that here," is extremely powerful, more so than any written rules or policy manuals.
    ← ANDREW S. GROVE, former CEO, Intel Corp.

All the forces of corporate culture are set against change.
    ← BRUCE HENDERSON, former CEO, Boston Consulting Group

Strong corporate cultures, like strong family cultures, come from within, and they are built by individual leaders, not consultants.
    ← CRAIG R. HICKMAN AND MICHAEL A. SILVA, president and CEO, Bennett Enterprises, and authors, *Creating Excellence: Managing Corporate Culture, Strategy and Change in the New Age*

I don't know about management techniques as such. I only know about engineering and people. The most important thing is the respect for people within the corporation, and so it's incumbent on the managers to create an environment within a corporation in which all employees are encouraged to take initiatives in carrying out the work, and doing the work with pleasure.
    ← SOICHIRO HONDA, founder, Honda Motors

If you believe that ten guys in pin-striped suits are back in kindergarten class playing with building blocks, you'll get a rough picture of what life in a corporation is like.
    ← LEE IACOCCA, former chairman, Chrysler Corp.

As long as people do their jobs well, I see no reason why they shouldn't have as much fun as they possibly can.
    ← ANDY JACOBS, cofounder, Jacobs Bros. Bagels

Culture is your number-one priority.
  —HERB KELLEHER, founder, chairman, and CEO, Southwest Airlines

You can be playful when everybody feels they're just as important as the next person. The reason you're not throwing a Nerf ball around is not that you're not playful; it's fear of retribution from somebody higher up. So if you can break down that barrier, everybody not only feels comfortable throwing the Nerf ball but coming up with ideas.
  —DAVID M. KELLEY, founder and CEO, IDEO

I favor a very democratic, open egalitarian atmosphere combined with a slightly mysterious, benevolent authority.
  —FRITZ MAYTAG, president, Anchor Brewing Co.

If you're working in a company that is NOT enthusiastic, energetic, creative, clever, curious, and just plain fun, you've got troubles, serious troubles.
  —TOM PETERS, author and consultant

Corporate culture sounds like the province of Bank of America and Federal Express. Guess again. Culture counts even for the one-principal consultancy that's supported by a part-time administrative assistant. The spirit, energy, and professionalism of that part-timer sets the tone for your service offering.
  —TOM PETERS

Nothing reveals more of what a company really cares about than its stories and legends .... Listening to a company's stories is the surest route to determining its real priorities and who symbolizes them.
  —TOM PETERS AND NANCY AUSTIN, authors and consultants

Elitism is an expensive salve that doesn't work. You thrive by having smart, dedicated people. Don't ever think you can divide the company into haves and have-nots, thinkers and doers.
  —FRANK POPOFF, CEO, Dow Chemical Co.

The deadlines, finish lines and fast-food lines are going to be removed, and we are going to see a new dawning inside the corporate culture, a dawning of wisdom, which is the ability to take knowledge and process it to make it something greater.

   —JOEY REIMAN, CEO, BrightHouse

There has been an enormous amount of pain and trauma. And the culture's not completely changed yet.

   —J. PHILIP SAMPER, former vice chairman and executive officer, Eastman Kodak, and cofounder, Gabriel Venture Partners

Sitting up here in Stamford, there's no way I can affect what an employee is doing in Texas, Montana, or Maine. Making speeches and sending letters just doesn't do it. You need a culture and peer pressure that spells out what is acceptable and isn't and why.

   —ANDREW SIGLER, chairman, Champion International Corporation

We look at the company, the products, and the internal culture as a continuum. To the extent that we are living the vision, mission, and values, the more successful we will be financially.

   —GREG STELTENPOHL, cofounder and former CEO, Odwalla, Inc.

Boundaryless behavior is a way of life here. People really do take ideas from A to B. And if you take an idea and share it, you are rewarded. In the old culture, if you had an idea you'd keep it. Sharing it with someone else would have been stupid, because the bureaucracy would have made him the hero, not you.

   —JACK WELCH, chairman and CEO, General Electric

We decide to create an open and dialogue-intensive corporate culture. This generates creativity and motivation and brings out entrepreneurs at all levels. This is the true power and success of Bertelsmann.

   —MARK WOESSNER, CEO, Bertelsmann Group

Creativity

Every good manager knows that our greatest natural resource is human creativity.
> ━MARY CUNNINGHAM AGEE, founder and executive director, Nurturing Network

The creative person wants ... to know about all kinds of things: ancient history, nineteenth century mathematics, current manufacturing techniques, flower arranging, and hog futures. Because he never knows when these ideas might come together to form a new idea.
> ━CARL ALLY, founder, Ally & Gargano Advertising

The amount a person uses his imagination is inversely proportional to the amount of punishment he will receive for using it.
> ━ANONYMOUS (workshop participant)

I get the facts, I study them patiently, I apply imagination.
> ━BERNARD BARUCH, American financier and presidential advisor

Properly practiced creativity can make one ad do the work of ten.
> ━WILLIAM BERNBACH, cofounder, DDB Needham Advertising

Curiosity about life in all of its aspects, I think, is still the secret of great creative people.
> ━LEO BURNETT, founder, Leo Burnett Advertising

Creative experiences can be produced regularly, consistently, almost daily in people's lives. [But] it requires enormous personal security and openness and a spirit of adventure.
> ━STEPHEN COVEY, consultant and author, *The 7 Habits of Highly Effective People*

Creative people have much more confidence in their imaginative leaps, in their intuition.
> ━LAUREL CUTLER, vice chairman, FCB/Leber Katz Partners

The need to be right all the time is the biggest bar to new ideas. It is better to have enough ideas for some of them to be wrong than to be always right by having no ideas at all.

    —EDWARD DE BONO, **creativity writer and trainer**

To invent, you need a good imagination and a pile of junk.

    —THOMAS A. EDISON, **American inventor**

Being creative doesn't necessarily mean reinventing the wheel. Small acts of creativity can be amazingly effective. And they tend to accumulate and gather momentum.

    —SETH GODIN, **founder and president, Yoyodyne Entertainment, and Vice President, Direct Marketing, Yahoo!**

Clearly no group can as an entity create ideas. Only individuals can do this. A group of individuals may, however, stimulate one another in the creation of ideas.

    —ESTILL I. GREEN, **VP, Bell Telephone Laboratories**

Big ideas happen when people build on each other's ideas.

    —DAVID M. KELLEY, **founder and CEO, IDEO**

Where there is an open mind, there will always be a frontier.

    —CHARLES F. KETTERING, **president, General Motors Research Corp., and cofounder, Sloan-Kettering Institute for Cancer Research**

There are two keys to being creatively productive. One is not being daunted by fear of failure. The other is sheer perseverance.

    —MARY-CLAIRE KING, **pioneer in human genetics**

Ideas need time [to develop], but [people] also need independence and latitude to be creative.

    —TOM KOULOPOULOS, **CEO, Delphi Group**

Creativity is a highfalutin word for the work I have to do between now and Tuesday.

    —RAY KROC, **chairman, McDonald's**

Sometimes the best way to heighten creativity is to stay out of the light.

—ALEXANDER KROLL, CEO, Young and Rubicam

Remember Raymond Rubicam's edict, "Resist the usual." The only way to achieve this is to pour a strategy through an individual so it comes out personal.

—ALEXANDER KROLL

Creativity can solve almost any problem. The creative act, the defeat of habit by originality, overcomes everything.

—GEORGE LOIS, founder, Lois/EJL Advertising

The key question isn't "what fosters creativity"? But it is "why in God's name isn't everyone creative"?

—ABRAHAM MASLOW, psychologist and author, *Maslow on Management*

Originality is the one thing which unoriginal minds cannot feel the use of.

—JOHN STUART MILL, economist

If I have a thousand ideas and only one turns out to be good, I am satisfied.

—ALFRED NOBEL, inventor of dynamite and founder, Nobel Prize

If it doesn't sell, it isn't creative.

—DAVID OGILVY, cofounder, Ogilvy & Mather Advertising

The best ideas come as jokes. Make your thinking as funny as possible.

—DAVID OGILVY

The difference between a top-flight creative man and the hack is his ability to express powerful meanings indirectly.

—VANCE PACKARD, author, *The Hidden Persuaders*

There's no evidence that you can keep an organization creative, although I think it is possible with a lot of energy and time.
—WALTER ULMER, president, Center for Creative Leadership

The things we fear most in organizations—fluctuations, disturbances, imbalances—are the primary sources of creativity.
—MARGARET J. WHEATLEY, consultant and author, *Leadership and the New Science*

Creative people have the ability to see new patterns and develop new approaches, theories, products, services that only after the fact seem obvious to everyone.
—JOHN WOODS, president, CWL Publishing Enterprises

Numerous studies demonstrate that people can be motivated to creativity simply with the addition of an instruction to "be creative."
—RICHARD SAUL WURMAN, developer, Insight Travel Guides

 *Criticism*

Sandwich every bit of criticism between two layers of praise.
—MARY KAY ASH, founder, Mary Kay Cosmetics

We consider our customers a part of our organization, and we want them to feel free to make any criticism they see fit in regard to our merchandise or service.
—L.L. BEAN, founder, L.L. Bean Co.

Make sure you have someone in your life from whom you can get reflective feedback.
—WARREN BENNIS, founder and chair, Leadership Institute, University of Southern California

I do not resent criticism, even when, for the sake of emphasis, it parts for the time with reality.
—WINSTON CHURCHILL, former Prime Minister, Great Britain

To avoid criticism, do nothing, say nothing, be nothing.
—ELBERT HUBBARD, founder, Roycroft Press, and publisher, *The Fra* and *The Philistine*

Words wound. But as a veteran of twelve years in the United States Senate, I happily attest that they do not kill.
—LYNDON B. JOHNSON, U.S. President

Honest criticism is hard to take, particularly from a relative, a friend, an aquaintance, or a stranger.
—FRANKLIN P. JONES, former CEO, American Management Association

If I care to listen to every criticism, let alone act on them, then this shop may as well be closed for all other businesses. I have learned to do my best, and if the end result is good then I do not care for any criticism, but if the end result is not good, then even the praise of ten angels would not make the difference.
—ABRAHAM LINCOLN, U.S. President

Management is destructively critical when mistakes kill initiative, and it's essential that we have many people with initiative if we are to continue to grow.
—WILLIAM MCKNIGHT, former Chairman, 3M Corp.

Never criticize until the person is convinced of your unconditional confidence in their abilities.
—JOHN ROBINSON, football coach, University of Southern California, and author, *Coach to Coach: Business Lessons from the Locker Room*

It is not the critic who counts, nor the man who points out how the strong man stumbles or where the doers of deeds could have done better.
—THEODORE ROOSEVELT, U.S. President

I have yet to find the man, however exalted his station, who did not do better work and put forth grater effort under a spirit of approval than under a spirit of criticism.

— CHARLES M. SCHWAB, former CEO, Bethlehem Steel

If you're going to be a bridge, you've got to be prepared to be walked upon.

— ROY A. WEST, former mayor, Richmond, VA

You can't let praise or criticism get to you. It's a weakness to get caught up in either one.

— JOHN WOODEN, former basketball coach, UCLA

Customers

The CEO has to play a person role in strategic planning, but my No. 1 personal priority is to have personal contacts with our customers.

— WILLIAM J. AVERY, chairman, CEO, and director, Crown, Cork & Seal Company, Inc.

A customer is the most important person ever in this office—in person or by mail. A customer is not dependent on us, we are dependent on him. A customer is not an interruption to our work, he is the purpose of it. We are not doing him a favor by serving him, he is doing us a favor by giving us the opportunity to do so. A customer is not someone to argue or match wits with. Nobody ever won an argument with a customer. A customer is a person who brings us his wants. It is our job to handle them profitably to him and to ourselves.

— L.L. BEAN CREDO

The first time customer research is done, executives frequently are surprised by the sizeable percentage of customers who defect for service-related reasons.

> ━LEONARD L. BERRY, director, Center for Retailing Studies, editor, *Arthur Andersen Retailing Issues Letter*, former president, American Marketing Association, and author, *Discovering the Soul of Service: The Nine Drivers of Sustainable Business Success*

The next time you face a customer who has every right to be upset, say something like this: 'I don't blame you for feeling as you do. If I were you, I'd feel exactly the same way. What would you like for me to do?' These are magical, healing words.

> ━H. JACKSON BROWN, JR., author, *Life's Little Instruction Book*

Don't just anticipate your customer's future needs. Create them.

> ━DANIEL BURRUS, founder and president, Burrus Research Associates, Inc., and author, *Technotrends*

Customer satisfaction is the most important issue to me, and if you really believe that, then you've got to tie it to your reward system, to your management practices, and we do. ... We measure customer satisfaction in every way imaginable.

> ━JOHN CHAMBERS, CEO, Cisco Systems, Inc.

We're not marketing to the customer—the customer is acting as a styling consultant to us.

> ━SANJAY CHOUDHURI, director of mass customization, Levi Strauss & Co.

Worry about being better; bigger will take care of itself. Think one customer at a time and take care of each one the best way you can.

> ━GARY COMER, founder, Lands' End

Both suppliers and customers must be treated as partners and collaborators, jointly looking for ways to improve efficiency across the entire spectrum of the value chain, not just in their respective businesses.

> ━MICHAEL DELL, founder and chairman, Dell Computer

[Enhancing the customer experience] is what drives company success. We explained how we were going to measure it. And we made it the basis of everyone's profit-sharing and incentive-compensation plan.

— MICHAEL DELL, founder and chairman, Dell Computer

The customer generates nothing. No customer asked for electric lights.

— W. EDWARDS DEMING, consultant and author, *Out of the Crisis*

Those who enter to buy, support me. Those who come to flatter, please me. Those who complain, teach me how I may please others so that more will come. Only those hurt me who are displeased but do not complain.

— MARSHALL FIELD, founder, Marshall Field Department Stores

It is not the employer who pays wages—he only handles the money. It is the customer who pays the wages.

— HENRY FORD, founder, Ford Motor Company

High quality means pleasing customers not just protecting them from annoyance.

— DAVID GARVIN, professor, Harvard Business School

It is the customer, and the customer alone, who casts the vote that determines how big any company should be.

— CRAWFORD H. GREENEWALT, former president, DuPont

You should never sacrifice humanity for speed.

— JOE GREULICH, director of MIS, Roberts Express

Reengineering posits a radical new principle: that the design of work must be based not on hierarchical management and the specialization of labor but on end-to-end processes and the creation of value for the customer.

— MICHAEL HAMMER, consultant and coauthor, *Reengineering the Corporation*

Increasingly, the key to success in our kind of business is being invited in by a potential customer to be part of a multifunctional product-development team.

⬩STEPHEN E. HARDIS, CEO, Eaton Corporation

Employees must be with Heath at least three years before they can answer the phone. The policy ensures that customers are greeted by someone who knows the ropes. It's had a very positive effect.

⬩JANICE HEATH, founder and CEO, Heath Corp.

All of management's efforts for *kaizen* boil down to two words: customer satisfaction.

⬩MASAAKI IMAI, consultant and author, *Kaizen*

Customer needs do not remain static. There is no such thing as a permanent list of customers' needs.

⬩JOSEPH M. JURAN, consultant and founder, The Juran Institute

Consumers are statistics. Customers are people.

⬩STANLEY MARCUS, cofounder, Neiman-Marcus Department Stores

You have to understand where your customers are driving their business and then translate that into the things you have to do.

⬩MICHAEL MARKS, president, Indian River Consulting Group Inc.

Those serving customers must be longer range in time and longer range in space.... Why is this? It's because the relationships ... are very different when these customers are supposed to be kept for a century or two ... instead of for the short term.

⬩ABRAHAM MASLOW, psychologist and author, *Maslow on Management*

Customer loyalty begins with experience.

⬩REGIS MCKENNA, chairman, The McKenna Group

One of the most important lessons of business—the value of concentrating on the customers you have.

⬩TOM MONAGHAN, founder, Domino's Pizza

Yes, I sell people things they don't need. I can't, however, sell them something they don't want. Even with advertising. Even if I were of a mind to.

─JOHN O'TOOLE, chairman, Foote Cone & Belding

It is the service we are not obliged to give that people value the most.

─JAMES C. PENNEY, founder, J.C. Penney stores

The way employees treat customers reflects the manner in which they're treated by management.

─JAMES A. PERKINS, former president, Cornell University

Remember, some customers will want to be chauffeured, others will want the wheel themselves. Some will speed, others will take it slow. One way or another, all will be in the driver's seat. It's just a question of which companies will pay for the ride.

─FAYE RICE, columnist, *Fortune*

The business process starts with the customer. In fact, if it is not started with the customer, it all too many times abruptly ends with the customer.

─WILLIAM SCHERKENBACH, consultant and author

Consumption is the sole end and purpose of all production; and the interest of the producer ought to be attended to only so far as it may be necessary for promoting that of the consumer.

─ADAM SMITH, economist and author, *The Wealth of Nations*

We consumers ... are more experienced. Out tempers are shorter, and our patience is thinner. As consumers, we are becoming aware of our power—the power to pick up our toys and go home, or to go somewhere else to play.

─PACO UNDERHILL, founder and managing director, Envirosell, and author, *Why We Buy: The Science of Shopping*

The thing that lies at the foundation of positive change, the way I see it, is service to a fellow human being.

—LECH WALESA, former President, Poland

Exceed your customer's expectations. If you do they'll come back over and over. Give them what they want—and a little more. Let them know you appreciate them. Make good on all your mistakes, and don't make excuses—apologize. Stand behind everything you do. "Satisfaction guaranteed" will make all the difference

—SAM WALTON, founder, Wal-Mart

Never underestimate the power of apology [to your customers]. The importance of apologizing for unmet expectations cannot be overstated.

—RON ZEMKE, consultant and author, *Knock 'em Dead* Service series

 *Decision Making*

One of the problems in the United States, with government and business, is the very short-term, expedient approach to problems.

—WILLIAM AGEE, former CEO, Morris Knudsen

The fine art of executive decision consists in not deciding questions that are not now pertinent, in not deciding prematurely, in not making decisions that cannot be made effectively and in not making decisions that others should make.

—CHESTER I. BARNARD, author, *The Functions of the Executive* (1938)

Most of our executives make very sound decisions. The trouble is many have then not turned out to be right.

—DONALD BULLOCK, training director, C & P Telephone Company

When your values are clear to you, making decisions becomes easier.
— ROY DISNEY, vice-chairman, Walt Disney Company

Whenever you see a successful business, someone once made a courageous decision.
— PETER F. DRUCKER, consultant and renowned management author

If the wrong fork in the road is taken, all the progress we have made over the years will be swept away.
— DONALD EPHLIN, vice president, UAW

Columbus did not seek a new route to the Indies in response to a majority directive.
— MILTON FRIEDMAN, economist

Often you have to rely on your intuition.
— BILL GATES, cofounder and chairman, Microsoft

If Intel used people holding old-fashioned position power to make all its decisions, decisions would be made by people unfamiliar with the technology of the day.
— ANDREW S. GROVE, former CEO, Intel Corp.

It's easy to make good decisions when there are no options.
— ROBERT HALF, founder, Robert Half International

We try to make management decisions that, if everything goes right, will preclude future problems. But everything does not always go right, and managers therefore must be problem solvers as well as decision makers.
— DENNIS HAYES, CEO, Hayes Microcomputer Products, Inc.

If it's a good idea... go ahead and do it. It is much easier to apologize than it is to get permission.
— GRACE MURRAY HOPPER, rear admiral U.S. Navy, developer of COBOL

If I had to sum up in one word what makes a good manager, I'd say decisiveness. You can use the fanciest computers to gather the numbers, but in the end you have to set a timetable and act.

→LEE IACOCCA, former chairman, Chrysler Corp.

There may be times when the best decision is to do nothing.

→RAY JOSEPHS, president, Ray Josephs Associates

I could make dumb decisions every day for the short term, and it would look great this year or next year, but it sure as hell wouldn't look good for the long term.

→LAWRENCE KICHEN, chairman, Lockheed

The absence of alternatives clears the mind marvelously.

→HENRY KISSINGER, former Secretary of State

The fact is you'll never have all the information you need to make a decision—if you did, it would be a foregone conclusion, not a decision.

→DAVID MAHONEY, chairman, Charles A. Dana Foundation

No matter how deep a study you make, what you really have to rely on is your own intuition, and when it comes down to it, you really don't know what's going to happen until you do it.

→KONOSUKE MATSUSHITA, founder, Matsushita Electric Co.

Most managers are not capable of making decisions involving complex technological matters without help—lots of it.... The finest technical people on the job should have dual role: doing technical work and advising management.

→PHILIP W. METZGER, computer analyst and co-author, *Managing a Programming Project: People and Processes*

Be willing to make decisions. That's the most important quality in a good leader.

→GEORGE PATTON, World War II general

Facts, as such, never settled everything. They are working tools only. It is the implications that can be drawn from facts that count, and to evaluate these requires wisdom and judgement....
— CLARENCE B. RANDALL, chairman, Inland Steel

Our theory of management is that the time to get a decision doubles for every two levels of management; thus, parallel instead of serial decisions are best solutions.
— EBERHARDT RECHTIN, president, Aerospace Corporation

Don't make decisions and commitments ahead of time that you don't have to make.
— MILTON J. ROEDEL, manager, DuPont

In any moment of decision, the best thing you can do is the right thing, the next best thing is the wrong thing, and the worst thing you can do is nothing.
— THEODORE ROOSEVELT, U.S. President

Forced to choose among irrelevant alternatives, on the basis of misleading facts, and without the benefit of solid analysis, even the best judgment can do little but grope intuitively in the dark.
— CHARLES L. SCHULTZE, former Director, Office of Management and Budget

Encouraging worker ideas and participation in decision making is no longer just an option for American business. It is a necessity. Employees come to the workplace today with expectations that their recommendations will be given serious consideration.
— ROGER SMITH, former chairman, General Motors

Decisions must be made at the lowest possible level for management at the top to retain its effectiveness.
— SAXON TATE, managing director, Canada and Dominion Sugar

Make every decision as if you owned the whole company.
— ROBERT TOWNSEND, former CEO, Avis Rent-a-Car, and author, *Up the Organization*

Lying dead in the water and doing nothing is a comfortable alternative because it is without risk, but it is an absolutely fatal way to manager a business.

　—THOMAS J. WATSON, JR., son of founder and former chairman, IBM

We don't so much make decisions but, rather, understand situations and act in accordance with that understanding.

　—JOHN WOODS, president, CWL Publishing Enterprises

Determination

Bite off more than you can chew. Then chew it.

　—ANONYMOUS

Concentration is my motto—first honesty, then industry, then concentration.

　—ANDREW CARNEGIE, founder, U.S. Steel

Nothing in this world can take the place of persistence. Talent will not; nothing is more common than unsuccessful people with talent. Genius will not; unrewarded genius is almost a proverb. Education will not; the world is full of educated derelicts. Persistence and determination alone are omnipotent.

　—CALVIN COOLIDGE, U.S. President

Concentration is the key to economic results. No other principle of effectiveness is violated as constantly today as the basic principle of concentration.

　—PETER F. DRUCKER, consultant and renowned management author

I never did anything work doing by accident, nor did any of my inventions come by accident; they came by work.

— THOMAS A. EDISON, **American inventor**

Persistence is what makes the impossible possible, the possible likely, and the likely definite.

— ROBERT HALF, **founder, Robert Half International**

Never give up and never give in.

— HUBERT H. HUMPHREY, **former Senator and U.S. Vice President**

Keep on going, and the chances are that you will stumble on something, perhaps when you are least expecting it. I never heard of anyone stumbling on something sitting down.

— CHARLES F. KETTERING, **president, General Motors Research Corp., and cofounder, Sloan-Kettering Institute for Cancer Research**

The difference between the impossible and the possible lies in determination.

— TOMMY LASORDA, **former manager, Los Angeles Dodgers**

Winning isn't everything, but wanting to win is.

— VINCE LOMBARDI, **legendary coach, Green Bay Packers**

It requires a great deal of boldness and a great deal of caution to make a great fortune; and when you have got it, it requires ten times as much wit to keep it.

— MEYER ROTHSCHILD, **financier**

A man can do anything he wants to do in this world, at least if he wants to do it badly enough.

— EDWARD W. SCRIPPS, **founder, United Press International**

Work only a half a day. It makes no difference which half—the first 12 hours or the last 12 hours.

— KEMMONS WILSON, **founder, Holiday Inns**

⸎ *Discipline* ⸎

The boss ... must discipline himself not to act on problems his managers can solve, and never to act on problems when he is explicitly reviewing status.

— FREDERICK P. BROOKS, project manager, System/360 computers and OS/360 software, IBM, and author, *The Mythical Man-Month*

Shakespeare wrote his sonnets within a strict discipline, fourteen lines of iambic pentameter, rhyming in three quatrains and a couplet. Were his sonnets dull? Mozart wrote his sonatas within an equally rigid discipline—exposition, development, and recapitulation. Were they dull?

— DAVID OGILVY, cofounder, Ogilvy & Mather Advertising

For every disciplined effort there is a multiple reward.

— JIM ROHN, entrepreneur and author, *7 Strategies for Wealth and Happiness*

Discipline is the refining fire by which talent becomes ability.

— ROY L. SMITH, editor-in-chief, *The Christian Advocate*, and author, *Know Your Bible*

Discipline is the soul of an army. It makes small numbers formidable; procures success to the weak, and esteem to all.

— GEORGE WASHINGTON, U.S. President

In an organization, discipline as a concept is about maintaining order and doing work as prescribed. This is a positive idea. Disciplined employees can be depended to complete tasks properly and on time. This substantially reduces the need for any other kind of discipline.

— JOHN WOODS, president, CWL Publishing Enterprises

Diversity

Diversity can be determining factor in whether a cutomers purchases our products or an investor invests in our company. Prospective clients compare themselves and their commitment to diversity to ours. They look at our track record. They look at us. It is important that they are able to see themselves.
— TED CHILDS, JR., VP, Global Workforce Diversity, IBM

A Leader must possess credibility, imagination, enthusiasm, vision, foresight, a sense of timing, a passion for excellence and be willing to share.
— FRED DELUCA, founder, Subway Sandwiches and Salads

Generally, employees who file complaints of discrimination do so as a last resort.
— RUBYE FIELDS, former national president, Blacks in Government

Focusing on diversity goes beyond being simply the right thing to do. The ranks of customers, employees, and vendors are becoming more diverse, so we must embrace and foster diversity as a necessary key to success. Those who do not, regardless of the business they are in, will be left behind.
— DOUGLAS G. GEOGA, president, Hyatt Hotels Corp.

We wanted to train men and women to go into the highest ranks of technology. ... And we wanted them to be so well trained that the color of their skin would not make any difference.
— ELEANOR JOSAITIS, founder, Focus:Hope, a Detroit development organization

Diversity is a competitive advantage. Different people approach similar problems in different ways.
— RICH McGINN, CEO, Lucent

We are in a war for talent. And the only way you can meet your business imperatives is to have all people as part of your talent pool—here in the United States and around the world.
— RICH McGINN, CEO, Lucent

Companies will have to be accountable to women or risk decline. Companies will have to disclose their hiring, paying, and promoting practices regarding women.
— NANCY RAMSEY, president, Morning Star Imports

Too often the great decisions are originated and given form in bodies made up wholly of men, or so completely dominated by them that whatever of special value women have to offer is shunted aside without expression.
— ELEANOR ROOSEVELT, former First Lady

[What we need most is] more diversity of thinking. If everybody in the room is the same, you'll have a lot fewer arguments and a lot worse answers.
— IVAN SEIDENBERG, CEO, Bell Atlantic

I've never used the expression, "It's the right thing to do." I think it's a '60s expression. And doing this is no more right than upgrading the facilities.
— IVAN SEIDENBERG

Today, diversity must be defined in far broader and more inclusive terms, including age, ethnic origins, cultures, and personal style.
— TERRY SIMMONS, president, Simmons Associates

Some people believe that seeking diversity automatically leads to excellence, but I think focusing on excellence inevitably leads to diversity.
— WILLIAM C. STEERE, CEO, Pfizer

Diversity is much broader than affirmative action today. ... Our markets demand that we be diverse because we serve such a diverse population. Diversity is more than the right thing to do— it's a business imperative.

    —LORRAINE STIMMEL, executive vice president, diversity and work life, Bank of America

Education

If you think education is expensive, try ignorance.

    —DEREK BOK, former president, Harvard University

I deal with the obvious. I present, reiterate and glorify the obvious—because the obvious is what people need to be told.

    —DALE CARNEGIE, author, *How to Win Friends and Influence People*

When a subject becomes totally obsolete we make it a required course.

    —PETER F. DRUCKER, consultant and renowned management author

It is less-bright students who make the teachers teach better.

    —MALCOLM FORBES, former publisher, *Forbes* magazine

A dollar put into a book and a book mastered might change the whole course of a boy's life. It might easily be the beginning of the development of leadership that would carry the boy far in service to his fellow man.

    —HENRY FORD, founder, Ford Motor Company

We can't take a slipshod and easygoing attitude toward education in this country. And by "we" I don't mean "somebody else," but I mean me and I mean you. It is the future of our country—yours and mine—which is at stake.

↞HENRY FORD, II, grandson of founder and former chairman, Ford Motor Company

An inventor is an engineer who doesn't take his education too seriously.

↞CHARLES F. KETTERING, president, General Motors Research Corp., and cofounder, Sloan-Kettering Institute for Cancer Research

A study of the history of opinion is a necessary preliminary to the emancipation of the mind.

↞JOHN MAYNARD KEYNES, economist

While formal schooling is an important advantage, it is not a guarantee of success, nor is its absence a fatal handicap.

↞RAY KROC, founder, McDonald's

Learning and sex until rigor mortis.

↞MAGGIE KUHN, founder, Gray Panthers

Many employees see training in one of three ways: as a reward, as an investment, or as a way to get rid of someone. Few see it as an investment.

↞BOB PIKE, training specialist

Management will recognize the need for education and retraining when they realize that people are an asset and not an expense.

↞WILLIAM SCHERKENBACH, consultant and author

In the information age, people are the only real assets, and education is the key to quality, productivity, and sustained profitability.

↞JACK SCHNIZUS, quality system manager, Johnson Mathey Electronics

This, then is the basic meaning of a "learning organization"—an organization that is continually expanding its capacity to create its future.

←Peter Senge, consultant, speaker, and author, *The Fifth Discipline*

Basically the dominant competitive weapon of the 21st century will be the education and skills of the work force.

←Lester Thurow, former dean, MIT Sloan School of Management

Recently, I was asked if I was going to fire an employee who made a mistake that cost the company $600,000. No, I replied, I just spent $600,000 training him. Why would I want somebody to hire his experience?

←Thomas J. Watson, Jr., son of founder and former chairman, IBM

Efficiency

I would I could stand on a busy corner, hat in hand, and beg people to throw me all their wasted hours.

←Bernard Berenson, art critic, historian, art dealer, and author

Everyone doing their best is not sufficient.

←W. Edwards Deming, consultant and author, *Out of the Crisis*

What is the major problem? It is fundamentally the confusion between effectiveness and efficiency that stands between doing the right things and doing things right. There is surely nothing quite so useless as doing with great efficiency what should not be done at all.

←Peter F. Drucker, consultant and renowned management author

There is no doubt that the most competitive manufacturers are those who have learned to produce more with fewer people.

    —EDWARD HENNESSY, JR., former chairman, AlliedSignal Inc.

We've come a third of the way to regaining competitiveness by slashing costs and improving productivity, but clearly we have not done enough.

    —JERRY J. JASINOWSKI, senior VP, National Association of Manufacturers

The machines that are first invented to perform any particular movement are always the most complex, and succeeding artists generally discover that, with fewer wheels the same effects may be more easily produced.

    —ADAM SMITH, economist and author, *An Inquiry into the Nature and Causes of the Wealth of Nations*

Hundreds would never have known want if they had not first known waste.

    —CHARLES H. SPURGEON, (1834-1892), "Prince of Preachers"

The reason America is not competitive is not because of a disadvantage in direct costs such as labor or materials.... What's outrageous are the overhead costs.

    —PAUL STRASSMANN, former VP, Xerox, and business author

All organizations are at least 50 percent waste—waste people, waste effort, waste space and waste time.

    —ROBERT TOWNSEND, former CEO, Avis Rent-a-Car, and author, *Up the Organization*

Control your expenses better than your competition. This is where you can always find the competitive advantage. You can make a lot of mistakes and still recover if you run an efficient operation. Or you can be brilliant and still go out of business if you're too inefficient.

    —SAM WALTON, founder, Wal-Mart

Employment

When more and more people are thrown out of work, unemployment results.

— CALVIN COOLIDGE, U. S. President

Unemployment is rarely considered desirable except by those who have not experienced it.

— JOHN KENNETH GALBRAITH, economist and author

A corporation prefers to offer a job to a man who already has one, or doesn't immediately need one. The company accepts you if you are already accepted. To obtain entry into paradise, in terms of employment, you should be in a full state of grace.

— ALAN HARRINGTON, advertising executive and author, *Life in the Crystal Palace*

When you have 7 percent unemployed, you have 93 percent working.

— JOHN F. KENNEDY, U.S. President

Have you ever told a coal miner in West Virginia or Kentucky that what he needs is individual initiative to go out and get a job where there isn't any?

— ROBERT F. KENNEDY, former U.S. Attorney General and U.S. presidential candidate

I am also concerned about talent. I like to say, "The people with the best people win." But you and I know there just are not enough people, period!

— SHELLY LAZARUS, chairman and CEO, Ogilvy & Mather Advertising

If you have lower than a 10% turnover, there is a problem. And if you have higher than, say 20%, there is a problem.

— WILLIAM G. MCGOWAN, founder, MCI Communications

Enthusiasm

A mediocre idea that generates enthusiasm will go further than a great idea that inspires no one.

—MARY KAY ASH, founder, Mary Kay Cosmetics

Motivation will almost always beat mere talent.

—NORMAN AUGUSTINE, president and CEO, Lockheed Martin

If you can give your son or daughter only one gift, let it be enthusiasm.

—BRUCE BARTON, cofounder, BBDO Advertising

Flaming enthusiasm, backed by horse sense and persistence, is the quality that most frequently makes for success.

—DALE CARNEGIE, author, *How to Win Friends and Influence People*

Success is going from failure to failure without a loss of enthusiasm."

—WINSTON CHURCHILL, former Prime Minister, Great Britain

Enthusiasm is at the bottom of all progress. With it there is accomplishment. Without it there are only alibis.

—HENRY FORD, founder, Ford Motor Company

Great dancers are not great because of their technique; they're great because of their passion.

—MARTHA GRAHAM, founder, Martha Graham Dance Company

Study the unusually successful people you know, and you will find them imbued with enthusiasm for their work, which is contagious. Not only are they themselves excited about what they are doing, but they also get you excited.

—PAUL W. IVEY, author, *Successful Salesmanship*

I consider my ability to arouse enthusiasm among men the greatest asset I possess. The way to develop the best that is in a man is by appreciation and encouragement.

　—CHARLES M. SCHWAB, **former chairman, Bethlehem Steel**

A man can succeed at almost anything for which he has unlimited enthusiasm.

　—CHARLES M. SCHWAB

People are going to be most creative and productive when they're doing something they're really interested in. So having fun isn't an outrageous idea at all. It's a very sensible one.

　—JOHN SCULLEY, **former chairman, Apple Computer**

Entrepreneurs

Being in your own business is working 80 hours a week so that you can avoid working 40 hours a week for someone else.

　—RAMONA E. F. ARNETT, **president, Ramona Enterprises**

[Starting a company is] like walking on a high wire. You can only make it if you concentrate all your attention on getting to the other side.

　—JAMES BERNSTEIN, **founder, General Health Inc.**

The critical ingredient is getting off your butt and doing something. It's as simple as that. A lot of people have ideas, but there are few who decide to do something about them now. Not tomorrow. Not next week. But today. The true entrepreneur is a doer, not a dreamer.

　—NOLAN BUSHNELL, **founder, Atari**

Show me an entrepreneur without a vision and I'll show you an entrepreneur who needs a new PR firm. Just don't try and put your vision in the bank.

—JOHN CASE, editor, *Inc.* magazine

Innovation is the specific tool of entrepreneurs, the means by which they exploit change as an opportunity for a different business or a different service.

—PETER F. DRUCKER, consultant and renowned management author

When I think about what it takes to make a successful startup, I ask three questions: What am I doing to build value? Do I have the right team in place? And—in terms of using my own time and energy—am I the right person for my particular team? Of these, the second is the hardest to answer—because it requires you to be brutally honest about people who often are truly committed to getting your startup off the ground.

—MARY FURLONG, founder, ThirdAge Media

The five essential entrepreneurial skills for success: Concentration, Discrimination, Organization, Innovation, and Communication.

—MICHAEL E. GERBER, founder, Gerber Business Development Corporation, chairman of The E-Myth Academy, and author, *The E-Myth Revisited*

Owner-run companies are often run in an arbitrary, dictatorial way. In fact, often that is what limits [their] growth.

—ANDREW S. GROVE, former CEO, Intel

If you want to be an entrepreneur, be sure that your aim is to be free to do something well. To leave a footprint in the sands of time. And be sure you give your employees the freedom to make contributions, to earn rewards—and even make mistakes.

—WILSON HARRELL, founder of over 100 companies and past publisher, *Inc.* magazine

An as entrepreneurial startup company you look at the business like a racer doing a sprint. But as a company gets successful, you've got to get your people to realize that it's a marathon they're in.

　　—TRIP HAWKINS, **president, Electronics Arts, Inc.**

Good management and entrepreneurship are not synonymous.

　　—JAMES L. HAYES, **former president, American Management Association**

The lack of realistic guidelines for entrepreneurial decision making … is a major reason large corporations find the creation of new ventures vexing.

　　—ROSABETH MOSS KANTOR AND WILLIAM H. FONVILLE, **consultants, professors, and business writers**

Entrepreneurs are simply those who understand that there is little difference between obstacle and opportunity and are able to turn both to their advantage.

　　—VICTOR KIAM, **CEO, Remington Products**

The entrepreneurial approach is not a sideline at 3M. It is the heart of our design for growth.

　　—LEWIS LEHR, **former CEO, 3M**

The difference between the great and good societies and the regressing, deteriorating societies is largely in terms of the entrepreneurial opportunity and the number of people in the society.

　　—ABRAHAM MASLOW, **psychologist and author,** *Maslow on Management*

We are shifting from a managerial society to an entrepreneurial society.

　　—JOHN NAISBITT, **former executive with IBM and Eastman Kodak, and author,** *Megatrends*, *Global Paradox*, **and** *High Tech/High Touch*

I'd rather have a class A entrepreneur with a class B idea than a class B entrepreneur with a class A idea.

　　—GIFFORD PINCHOT, III, **consultant and author,** *Intrapreneuring*

To be successful as an entrepreneur, you have to build a company around your whole life, not just the business aspect.
 —WARREN RODGERS, CEO, Computer Specialists, Inc.

Entrepreneurs are needed not only to start new business ventures … but also to put life into existing companies, especially large ones.
 —ANDERS WALL, CEO, Beijerinvest

Ethics

Honesty is the cornerstone of all success, without which confidence and ability to perform shall cease to exist.
 —MARY KAY ASH, founder, Mary Kay Cosmetics

I think it's unethical to take money for poor quality performance.
 —ALVIN BURGER, founder, "Bugs" Burger Bug Killers

Business leaders today can't shrink from their obligation to set a moral example.
 —WILLARD C. BUTCHER, former chairman, The Chase Manhattan Corp.

Shelving hard decisions is the least ethical course.
 —ADRIAN CADBURY, chairman, Cadbury Schweppes

I don't care how many martinis anyone has with lunch. But I do care who picks up the check.
 —JIMMY CARTER, U.S. President

I haven't committed a crime. What I did was fail to comply with the law.
 —DAVID DINKINS, former Mayor, New York City

Start with what is right rather than what is acceptable.
> —PETER F. DRUCKER, consultant and renowned management author

At Medtronic we don't mix religion and business, but we certainly do not shy away from the spiritual side of our work and the deeper meaning of our mission to save lives.
> —BILL GEORGE, CEO, Medtronic

Everybody has a little bit of Watergate in him.
> —BILLY GRAHAM, American evangelist

As a small businessperson, you have no greater leverage than the truth.
> —PAUL HAWKEN, cofounder, Smith & Hawken

If managers are careless about basic things—telling the truth, respecting moral codes, proper professional conduct—who can believe them on other issues?
> —JAMES L. HAYES, former president, American Management Association

Ethics must begin at the top of an organization. It is a leadership issue and the chief executive must set the example.
> —EDWARD L. HENNESSY, JR., former chairman, Allied Signal (now Honeywell)

First, there is the law. It must be obeyed. But the law is the minimum. You must act ethically.
> —IBM CREDO

The strength of our commitment to a high level of ethical [business] behavior ... has deteriorated almost in direct proportion to declining societal values.
> —ROBERT L. KOCH, VP personnel, Bally

The purpose of Motorola is to honorably serve the community by providing products and services of superior quality at a fair price to our customers; to do this so as to earn an adequate profit which is required for the enterprise to grow, and by so doing provide the opportunity for our employees and shareholders to achieve reasonable personal objectives.
— FROM "FOR WHICH WE STAND: A STATEMENT OF PURPOSE, PRINCIPLES, AND ETHICS," MOTOROLA

The market is full of hucksters, promoting quick-fix ethics programs.
— MARK J. PASTIN, director, Lincoln Center for Ethics

One player practicing sportsmanship is far better than fifty preaching it.
— KNUTE ROCKNE, former football coach, Notre Dame University

If it doesn't follow the Golden Rule, I don't want to participate in it. We've never made any money bad-mouthing anyone else.
— MORRIS SIEGEL, founder, Celestial Seasonings

The art of ethical management lies in unmixing the "grey" areas to achieve clarity in resolution of ethical dilemmas.
— SHELDON S. STEINBERG, Sr. VP, University Research Corp.

When I want to buy up any politicians I always find the anti-monopolists the most purchasable. They don't come so high.
— WILLIAM H. VANDERBILT, American financier

Despite the codes of ethics, the ethics programs, and the special departments—*corporations* don't make the ultimate decisions about ethics. Ethical choices are made by *individuals*.
— M. EUEL WADE, JR., Sr. VP, Southern Services Corp.

Excellence

Quality is the degree of excellence at an acceptable price and the control of variability at an acceptable cost.
  —ROBERT A. BROH, author, *Managing for Quality*

You can't build a reputation on what you are going to do.
  —HENRY FORD, founder, Ford Motor Company

Some people have greatness thrust upon them. Very few have excellence thrust upon them.
  —JOHN GARDNER, founder, Common Cause, and author, *Excellence*

An excellent plumber is infinitely more admirable than an incompetent philosopher. The society that scorns excellence in plumbing just because plumbing is a humble activity, and tolerates shoddiness in philosophy because it is an exalted activity, will have neither good plumbing nor good philosophy. Neither its pipes nor its philosophy will hold water.
  —JOHN GARDNER

There is natural aristocracy among men. The grounds of this are virtue and talent.
  —THOMAS JEFFERSON, U.S. President

I think we have to appreciate that we're alive for only a limited period of time, and we'll spend most of our lives working. That being the case, I believe one of the most important priorities is to do whatever we do as well as we can. We should take pride in that.
  —VICTOR KIAM, CEO, Remington Products

The achievement of excellence can only occur if the organization promotes a culture of creative dissatisfaction.
  —LAWRENCE MILLER, president, Miller Consulting Group, and author, *Barbarians to Bureaucrats* and *From Management to Leadership*

We found that the most exciting environments, that treated people very well, are also tough a nail. There is no bureaucratic mumbo-jumbo ... excellent companies provide two things simultaneously: tough environments and very supportive environments.

— Tom Peters, author and consultant

You must publicly and repeatedly state the importantance of people to organizational success. If senior management doesn't affirm the importance of people, little else will happen.

— Jeffrey Pfeffer, professor, Stanford Business School, and author, *Competitive Advantage Through People*

If you do things well, do them better. Be daring, be first be different, be just.

— Anita Roddick, founder, The Body Shop

If you don't do it excellently, don't do it at all. Because if it's not excellent, it would be profitable or fun, and if you're not in business for fun and profit, what the hell are you doing here?

— Robert Townsend, former president, Avis Rent-a-Car, and author, *Up the Organization*

Excellence can be attained if you:
• Care more than others think is wise
• Risk more than others think is safe
• Dream more than others think is practical
• Expect more than others think is possible

— Unknown

If you want to achieve excellence, you can get there today. As of this second, quit doing less-than-excellent work.

— Thomas Watson, Sr., founder, IBM

Expectations

Set your expectations high; find men and women whose integrity and values you respect; get their agreement on a course of action; and give them your ultimate trust.

➤ JOHN AKERS, former CEO, IBM

Vote for the man who promises least; he'll be the least disappointing.

➤ BERNARD BARUCH, American financier and presidential advisor

If you expect nothing, you're apt to be surprised.

➤ MALCOLM FORBES, former publisher, *Forbes* magazine

What is remarkable for one person may not be for another. It depends on what your customer has come to expect from your business.

➤ GODFREY HARRIS, president, Harris/Ragan Management Group, and author, *Talk Is Easy!* and *Don't Take Our Word for It!*

Expect everything, and anything seems nothing. Expect nothing, and anything seems everything.

➤ SAMUEL HAZO, professor emeritus of English, Duquesne University, and State Poet of the Commonwealth of Pennsylvania

What we are doing is satisfying the American public. That's our job. I always say we have to give most of the people what they want most of the time. That's what they expect from us.

➤ WILLIAM PALEY, founder, CBS

Give a lot, expect a lot, and if you don't get it, prune.

➤ TOM PETERS, author and consultant

The shortest period of time lies between the minute you put some money away for a rainy day and the unexpected arrival of rain.

➤ JANE BRYANT QUINN, financial writer and advisor

The problem is not that there are problems. The problem is expecting otherwise and thinking that having problems is a problem.
—THEODORE RUBIN, author, several books on self-help psychology

High expectations are the key to everything.
—SAM WALTON, founder, Wal-Mart

If you always expect the unexpected, you'll seldom be disappointed.
—JOHN WOODS, president, CWL Publishing Enterprises

 *Experience*

The taste of defeat has a richness of experience all its own.
—BILL BRADLEY, former Senator and NBA basketball player

We are too busy looking forward to the next deadline to see what we are carrying with us from the past.
—MARILYN DARLING, president, Signet Consulting Group

After 40, one's face begins to tell more than one's tongue.
—MALCOLM FORBES, former publisher, *Forbes* magazine

I'm not a genius. I'm just a tremendous bundle of experience.
—R. BUCKMINSTER FULLER, inventor and idea provocateur

We learn simply by the exposure of living. Much that passes for education is not education at all but ritual. The fact is that we are being educated when we know it least.
—DAVID P. GARDNER, president, William and Flora Hewlett Foundation, and co-author, *A Nation at Risk: The Imperative for Educational Reform*

In the business world, everyone is paid in two coins: cash and experience. Take the experience first; the cash will come later.
— HAROLD GENEEN, **former CEO, IT&T**

Experience enables you to recognize a mistake when you make it again.
— FRANKLIN P. JONES, **former CEO, American Management Association**

The genius of America is production; and a large percentage of our productive enterprises are headed by men who have come up from the worker's bench.
— WILLIAM S. KNUDSEN, **former president, General Motors**

If somebody has not been knocked around by life, I get concerned, not only about his judgment but about his resiliency. Experience, if it doesn't kill you, teaches you how to bounce back.
— DAVID MAHONEY, **chairman, Charles A. Dana Foundation**

When it comes time to teach, teach from your experience. Go out and do, learn from the doing, then teach from the knowing.
— PETER MCWILLIAMS, **author and entrepreneur**

It's too costly today to learn from your own experience. You not only learn much faster, but it is also much cheaper to learn from other people's experiences.
— ROBERT L. MONTGOMERY, **president, R. L. Montgomery & Associates**

Everyone is a prisoner of his own experiences. No one can eliminate prejudices—just recognize them.
— EDWARD R. MURROW, **broadcast journalist**

A couple of hours in a hot kitchen can teach you as much about business and management as the latest books on reengineering or total quality management.
— TOM PETERS, **author and consultant**

You gain strength, courage, and confidence by every experience in which you really stop to look fear in the face.

　　✦ELEANOR ROOSEVELT, former First Lady

Good judgment comes from experience, and experience comes from poor judgment.

　　✦SIGN IN A LUMBER YARD

In school, you get a theoretical education, but to really learn the business, you have to do it.

　　✦ROSA SUGRANES, president, Iberia Tiles Corporation

If the second and third generations could profit by the experience of the first generation, we would not be having some of the troubles we have today.

　　✦HARRY S. TRUMAN, U.S. PRESIDENT

From misunderstanding comes experience.

　　✦JOHN WOODS, president, CWL Publishing Enterprises

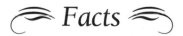

⨳ Facts ⨳

When you approach a problem, strip yourself of preconceived opinions and prejudice, assemble and learn the facts of the situation, make the decision which seems to you the most honest, and then stick to it.

　　✦CHESTER BOWLES, cofounder, Benton and Bowles advertising firm, Governor of Connecticut (1948-1950), and member of the U.S. House of Representatives (1959-1960)

The most important thing in science is not so much to obtain new facts as to discover new ways of thinking about them.

　　✦SIR WILLIAM BRAGG, British scientist and winner, the Nobel Prize for Physics (1915)

Anyone who says businessmen deal only in facts, not fiction, has never read old five-year projections.

→ MALCOLM FORBES, former publisher, *Forbes* magazine

The man who questions opinions is wise; the man who quarrels with facts is a fool.

→ FRANK A. GARBUTT, cinematographer, manager, and VP, Los Angeles Athletic Club (1920s)

A concept is stronger than a fact.

→ CHARLOTTE PERKINS GILMAN, founder, *The Forerunner* (magazine), and author, *Women and Economics*

No talent in management is worth more than the ability to master facts—not just any facts, but the ones that provide the best answers. ... The process can be laborious—which is why it is so often botched.

→ ROBERT HELLER, editor, *Management Today*

In quality control, we try as far as possible to make our various judgments based on the facts, not on guesswork. Our slogan is "Speak with facts."

→ KATSUYA HOSOTANI, author, *Japanese Quality Concepts: An Overview* and *The Qc Problem-Solving Approach: Solving Workplace Problems the Japanese Way*

Facts are friendly. Facts that tend to reinforce what you are doing and give you a warm glow are nice, because they help in terms of psychic reward. Facts that raise alarms are equally friendly, because they give you clues about how to respond, how to change, where to spend the resources.

→ IRWIN MILLER, CEO, Cummins Engine Co.

A single fact can spoil a good argument.

→ UNKNOWN

By all means, let's not confuse ourselves with the facts!

➤UNKNOWN

Facts Tell; Stories Sell!

➤UNKNOWN

People never knowingly ignore the facts.

➤JOHN WOODS, president, CWL Publishing Enterprises

 *Failure*

There is a price for success but there is also a price for failure. Given the choice, the price of success clearly has the best return on investment.

➤MICHAEL ANGIER, founder, Success Networks International

People fail forward to success.

➤MARY KAY ASH, founder, Mary Kay Cosmetics

Failing organizations are usually over-managed and under-led.

➤WARREN G. BENNIS, founder and chair, Leadership Institute, University of Southern California

It's not necessary to fear the prospect of failure but to be determined not to fail.

JIMMY CARTER, U.S. President

Success in 99 percent failure.

SOICHIRO HONDA, founder, Honda Motor Company

The guns and bombs, the rockets and the warships, all are symbols of human failure.

➤LYNDON B. JOHNSON, U.S. President

Failure is our most important product.
> ━ROBERT W. JOHNSON, JR., **former CEO, Johnson & Johnson**

Only those who dare to fail greatly can ever achieve greatly.
> ━ROBERT F. KENNEDY, **former U.S. Attorney General and U.S. presidential candidate**

Eleven Rules on How to Lose:
1. Stop taking risks.
2. Be content.
3. Never deviate from what the founder did.
4. Be inflexible.
5. Rely totally on research and experts.
6. Concentrate on competitors instead of your customers.
7. Put yourself—not the customer—first.
8. Solve administrative concerns first.
9. Let others do your thinking—for example, headquarters.
10. Rely on T-G-E ("That's Good Enough") and T-N-M-J ("That's Not My Job").
11. Rationalize slow growth.
> ━DON KEOUGH, **former president, Coca-Cola**

An inventor fails 999 times, and if he succeeds once, he's in. He treats his failures simply as practice shots.
> ━CHARLES F. KETTERING, **president, General Motors Research Corp., and cofounder, Sloan-Kettering Institute for Cancer Research**

The only time you don't want to fail is the last time you try.
> ━CHARLES F. KETTERING

Successful people are very lucky. Just ask any failure.
> ━MICHAEL LEVINE, **founder, Levine Communications Office and the Innovative Business Alliance, and author,** *Lessons at the Halfway Point*

In great attempts it is glorious even to fail.
> ━VINCE LOMBARDI, **legendary coach, Green Bay Packers**

Failures are like skinned knees—painful, but superficial.

➤ H. Ross Perot, founder, EDS and Perot Systems

Success has many mothers, but failure is a bastard.

➤ Unknown

Remember the two benefits of failure. First, if you do fail, you learn what doesn't work; and second, the failure gives you the opportunity to try a new approach.

➤ Roger von Oech, author, *A Whack on the Side of the Head*

We reward failure. I remember some guys came up with a lamp that didn't work, and we gave them all television sets. You have to do it, because otherwise people will be afraid to try things.

➤ Jack Welch, chairman and CEO, General Electric

The seeds of failure come from the fruit of our success.

➤ John Woods, president, CWL Publishing Enterprises

Free Enterprise

The gospel of wealth advocates leaving free the operation of laws of accumulation.

➤ Andrew Carnegie, founder, U.S. Steel

And no matter how radical Ralph Nader may sound, his is a highly conventional view of the "system." ... Nader believes in economic performance above all; he makes it the central touchstone of a good society.

➤ Peter F. Drucker, consultant and renowned management author

To the infantryman, his country's military might is only those bud-
dies he can see, and the equipment they have at hand; likewise, to
the wage-earner, free enterprise is primarily the way his boss treats
him and those around him.

　　━MALCOLM FORBES, former publisher, *Forbes* magazine

Exchange can bring about coordination without coercion.

　　━MILTON FRIEDMAN, economist

Is advertising moral? It is part and parcel of the American free
enterprise system... I challenge anybody to show any [economic]
system that has done as much for so many in so short time.

　　━MORRIS HITE, chair, 1950-1982, Tracy-Locke Advertising Agency
　　(now DDB Needham)

Agriculture, manufacture, commerce, and navigation, the four pil-
lars of our prosperity, are the most thriving when left most free to
individual enterprise.

　　━THOMAS JEFFERSON, U.S. President

One of the aspects of the free enterprise system is that you should
be allowed to succeed, and you should also be allowed to fail.

　　━REGINALD JONES, former chairman, General Electric

That some should be rich, shows that others may become rich, and
hence is just encouragement to industry and enterprise.

　　━ABRAHAM LINCOLN, U.S. President

Officially we revere free enterprise, initiative, and individuality.
Unofficially, we fear it.

　　━GEORGE LOIS, founder, Lois/EJL Advertising, and author, *The Art
　　of Advertising: George Lois on Mass Communication*

If the spirit of business adventure is dulled, this country will cease
to hold the foremost position in the world.

　　━ANDREW MELLON, founder, Aluminum Company of America
　　(Alcoa) and the Gulf Oil Company, cofounder, Union Steel Com-
　　pany and Union Trust Company

 Fulfillment

Never permit a dichotomy to rule your life, a dichotomy in which you hate what you do so you can have pleasure in your spare time. Look for a situation in which your work will give you as much happiness as your spare time.

> —EDWARD L. BERNAYS, "the father of Public Relations" and author, *Propaganda, Public Relations*, and *Crystallizing Public Opinion*

I'm the luckiest guy in the world in terms of what I do for a living. No one can tell me to do things I don't believe in or things I think are stupid.

> —WARREN BUFFET, chairman, Berkshire Hathaway

I feel sorry for the person who can't get genuinely excited about his work. Not only will he never be satisfied, but he will never achieve anything worthwhile.

> —WALTER CHRYSLER, founder, Chrysler Motors

I don't think anybody yet has invented a pastime that's as much fun, or keeps you as young, as a good job.

> —FREDERICK HUDSON ECKER, chairman, Metropolitan Life

I continue to find my greatest pleasure, and so my reward, in the work that precedes what the world calls success.

> —THOMAS A. EDISON, American inventor

The biggest mistake people make in life is not trying to make a living at doing what they most enjoy.

> —MALCOLM FORBES, former publisher, *Forbes* magazine

To love what you do and feel that it matters—how could anything be more fun?

> —KATHARINE GRAHAM, publisher, *The Washington Post*

There are three hungers that people are trying to feed throughout their lives. The first is to connect deeply with the creative spirit of life. The second hunger is to know and express your gifts and talents. The third hunger is to know that our lives matter. Fulfillment comes from feeding these three hungers.

➤ RICHARD LEIDER, founding partner, The Inventure Group

The road to happiness lies in two simple principles: find what it is that interests you and that you can do well, and when you find it put your whole soul into it—every bit of energy and ambition and natural ability you have.

➤ JOHN D. ROCKEFELLER, III, American financier and philanthropist

Far and away the best prize that life offers is the chance to work hard at work worth doing.

➤ THEODORE ROOSEVELT, U.S. President

An attitude to life which seeks fulfillment in the single-minded pursuit of wealth—in short, materialism—does not fit into this world, because it contains within itself no limiting principle, while the environment in which it is placed is strictly limited.

➤ E. F. SCHUMACHER, author, *Small Is Beautiful*

The man who does not work for the love of work, but only for money, is not likely to make money nor to find much fun in life.

➤ CHARLES M. SCHWAB, former CEO, Bethlehem Steel

I never worked a day in my life. It's not work when you love what you're doing.

➤ DAVID SHAKARIAN, founder, General Nutrition

Deals are my art form. Other people paint beautifully on canvas or write wonderful poetry. I like making deals, preferably big deals. That's how I get my kicks.

➤ DONALD TRUMP, chairman, The Trump Organization

Global Economy

Overseas operations used to be thought of as appendages or subsidiaries to help increase sales; now they're part of a network for accessing knowledge and human capital around the world.
— CHRISTOPHER BARTLETT, professor, Harvard Business School

The organization as we know it is becoming very porous and the whole sense of operating is becoming seven days a week, 24 hours a day, because we are global.
— JAMES CHAMPY, chairman, Perot Systems Consulting

We therefore consider it necessary that international exchanges should rest, as was the case before the great world misfortunes, on an indisputable basis bearing the mark of no particular country.
— CHARLES DE GAULLE, former President, France

What we call foreign affairs is no longer foreign affairs. It's a local affair. Whatever happens in Indonesia is important to Indiana. Whatever happens in any corner of the world has some effect on the farmer in Dickinson County, Kansas or on a worker in a factory.
— DWIGHT D. EISENHOWER, U.S. President

Without a global revolution in the sphere of human consciousness a more humane society will not emerge.
— VACLAV HAVEL, President, Czech Republic

With the proper flow of commerce across the borders of all countries, it is unnecessary for soldiers to march across those borders.
— THOMAS J. WATSON, SR., founder, IBM

American businesspeople have thought too small: They've focused almost solely on the United States and Europe. But for every person in on of these markets, there are three people in the developing world. What a missed opportunity!
— MUHAMMAD YUNUS, CEO, GrameenPhone Ltd.

Technology allows companies to hire people from anywhere. A U.S. security company, for example, can hire villagers to monitor its systems in homes and offices. What difference does it make if the person monitoring such a system is sitting in Illinois or India?
— MUHAMMAD YUNUS, CEO, GrameenPhone Ltd.

⪢ *Human Relations* ⪡

As a management consultant I have found that most of my clients spend more time talking about how to cope with problem employees, bosses, customers, and co-workers than about anything else.
— ROBERT M. BRAMSON, consultant and author, *Coping with Difficult People*, and coauthor, *The Art of Thinking*

When dealing with people, remember that you are not dealing with creatures of logic but with creatures of emotion.
— DALE CARNEGIE, author, *How to Win Friends and Influence People*

The most important ingredient we put into any relationship is not what we say or what we do, but what we are.
— STEPHEN COVEY, consultant and author, *The 7 Habits of Highly Effective People*

People who are constantly repressing, not transcending feelings toward a higher meaning find that it affects the quality of their relationships with others.
— STEPHEN COVEY

The strain and discouragement of frankly facing the complex tangle of motives at work in most human situations tempt everyone into the errors of oversimplification.
— HENRY S. DENNISON, founder, Dennison Corporation

In the few cases where we have been able to generate management energies we have generated rapid development. Development, in other words, is a matter of human energies rather than of economic wealth. And the generation and direction of human energies is the task of management. Management is the mover, and development is a consequence.

—PETER F. DRUCKER, consultant and renowned management author

Always listen to a man when he describes the faults of others. Ofttimes, most times, he's describing his own, revealing himself.

—MALCOLM FORBES, former publisher, *Forbes* magazine

The weak can never forgive. Forgiveness is the attribute of the strong.

—MOHANDAS K. GANDHI, leader, Indian independence movement

What you manage in business is people.

—HAROLD GENEEN, former CEO, IT&T

When it comes to people and their quirks, idiosyncracies, and personality flaws, the variety seems to be limitless. The manager's aim always remains the same: to keep these human beings from clogging up the workings of their group.

—ANDREW S. GROVE, former CEO, Intel Corp.

Giving people a little more than they expect is a good way to get back a lot more than you'd expect.

—ROBERT HALF, founder, Robert Half International

Am I not destroying my enemies when I make friends of them?

—ABRAHAM LINCOLN, U.S. President

First, all relationships are with yourself—and sometimes they involve other people. Second, the most important relationship in your life—the one you have, like it or not, until the day you die—is with yourself.

—PETER MCWILLIAMS, author and publisher

Understand that you, yourself, are no more than the composite picture of all your thoughts and actions. In your relationships with others, remember the basic and critically important rule: "If you want to be loved, be lovable. If you want respect, set a respectable example!"
— DENIS WAITLEY, founder, Management Development Institute, and author

All great questions of politics and economics come down in the last analysis to the decisions and action of individual men and women. They are questions of human relations, and we ought always to think about them in terms of men and women—the individual human beings who are involved in them.
— THOMAS J. WATSON, SR., founder, IBM

I know that you cannot hate other people without hating yourself.
— OPRAH WINFREY, talk show host and business owner

I believe that we all do the best we can in every situation. Understanding this, it helps me look with compassion on others, especially when I think they're screwing up.
— JOHN WOODS, president, CWL Publishing Enterprises

The Golden Rule is not something we have a choice about following. By definition we do unto others as we would have them do unto us—for good or ill.
— JOHN WOODS

Humility

If anything goes bad, I did it. If anything goes semi-good, we did it. If anything goes really good, then you did it. That's all it takes to get people to win football games for you.
— PAUL "BEAR" BRYANT, former football coach, University of Alabama

By humility I mean not the abjectness of a base mind, but a prudent care not to overvalue ourselves.

—NATHANIEL CREW (1633-1721), Bishop of Durham

My grandfather once told me that there were two kinds of people: those who do the work and those who take the credit. He told me to try to be in the first group; there was much less competition.

—INDIRA GANDHI, former Prime Minister, India

People who look down on other people don't end up being looked up to.

—ROBERT HALF, founder, Robert Half International

Never hire or promote in your own image. It is foolish to replicate your strength and idiotic to replicate your weakness. It is essential to employ, trust, and reward those whose perspective, ability, and judgment are radically different from yours. It is also rare, for it requires uncommon humility, tolerance, and wisdom.

—DEE W. HOCK, founder and CEO emeritus, VISA USA and VISA International

You don't need an MBA from Harvard to figure out how to lose money.

—ROYAL LITTLE, founder, Textron

Mental toughness is many things. It is humility because it behooves all of us to remember that simplicity is the sign of greatness and meekness is the sign of true strength. Mental toughness is spartanism with qualities of sacrifice, self-denial, dedication. It is fearlessness, and it is love.

—VINCE LOMBARDI, legendary coach, Green Bay Packers

Don't be humble. You're not that great.

—GOLDA MEIR, former Prime Minister, Israel

The challenge of leadership is to be strong, but not rude; be kind, but not weak; be bold, but not bully; be thoughtful, but not lazy; be humble, but not timid; be proud, but not arrogant; have humor, but without folly.

— JIM ROHN, entrepreneur and author, *7 Strategies for Wealth and Happiness*

The culture of a company starts at the top. It reflects the style of the leader. You have to use humility, create a motivating environment, mentor as well as manage

— MIKE SEASHOLS, president and CEO, USoft Corporation

It's important for me to get on the cafeteria line like everyone else.

— RALPH E. WARD, CEO, Cheseborough-Pond

There's no telling how far a person can go if he's willing to let other people take the credit.

— ROBERT WOODRUFF, former chairman, Coca-Cola

Humility is a wonderful trait. It reminds us it's not our fault whether we've succeeded in something or not.

— JOHN WOODS, president, CWL Publishing Enterprises

Early in life I had to choose between honest arrogance and hypocritical humility. I chose honest arrogance and have seen no occasion to change.

— FRANK LLOYD WRIGHT, architect

 *Ideas*

One of the greatest pains of human nature is the pain of a new idea.

— WALTER BAGEHOT, founding editor, *The Economist*

The human mind likes a strange idea as little as the body likes a strange protein and resists it with similar energy.

— WILLIAM H. BEVERIDGE, director, London School of Economics (1919-1937), and author

We like to test things ... no matter how good an idea sounds, test it first.

— HENRY BLOCK, founder, H&R Block

When fantasy turns you on, you're obligated to God and nature to start doing it right away.

— STEWART BRAND, cofounder, Global Business Network

When you try to formalize or socialize creative activity, the only sure result is commercial constipation.... The good ideas are all hammered out in agony by individuals, not spewed out by groups.

— CHARLES BROWDER, former president, Batten, Barton, Durstine, and Osborn (BBDO) Advertising

I have learned to respect ideas, wherever they come from. Often they come from clients. Account executives often have big creative ideas, regardless of what some writers think.

— LEO BURNETT, founder, Leo Burnett Advertising

The ideas I stand for are not mine. I borrowed them from Socrates. I swiped them from Chesterfield. I stole them from Jesus. And I put them in a book. If you don't like their rules, whose would you use?

— DALE CARNEGIE, author, *How to Win Friends and Influence People*

The value of an idea lies in the using of it.

— THOMAS A. EDISON, American inventor

A concept is stronger than a fact.

— CHARLOTTE PERKINS GILMAN, founder, *The Forerunner* (magazine), and author, *Women and Economics*

So many new ideas are at first strange and horrible though ultimately valuable that a very heavy responsibility rests upon those who would prevent their dissemination.

— J.B.S. HALDANE, professor of genetics, London University (1933-1937), and biometry, University College (1937-1957), and author, *The Causes of Evolution*

Acting on a good idea is better than just having a good idea.

— ROBERT HALF, founder, Robert Half International

To stay ahead, you must have your next idea waiting in the wings.

— ROSABETH MOSS KANTER, professor, Harvard Business School

In many ways ideas are more important than people—they are much more permanent.

— CHARLES F. KETTERING, president, General Motors Research Corp., and cofounder, Sloan-Kettering Institute for Cancer Research

Getting ideas is like shaving; if you don't do it every day, you're a bum.

— ALEXANDER KROLL, CEO, Young and Rubicam

Often the difference between a successful man and a failure is not one's better abilities or ideas, but the courage that one has to bet on his ideas, to take a calculated risk—and to act.

— MAXWELL MALTZ, plastic surgeon and author, *Psycho-Cybernetics* and *Zero-Resistance Selling*

I'm not impressed with the power of a corporate president. I am impressed with the power of ideas.

— KEN MASON, president, Quaker Oats

It's nice to say that knowledge is power, but of course, that's a bunch of hooey. Power is power. And, as a change agent, the power you've got is the power of new ideas.

— CLIVE MEANWELL, founder and CEO, Medicines Co.

It first appeared like a crazy idea. It turned out he had a great idea.

　　―J. RICHARD MUNRO, CEO, Time Inc.

Never hesitate to steal a good idea.

　　―AL NEUHARTH, founder, *USA Today*

You can judge your age by the amount of pain you feel when you come in contact with a new idea.

　　―JOHN NUVEEN, investment banker and founder, John Nuveen & Co. Inc.

I have always believed that good ideas will drive out bad ideas.

　　―BILL O'BRIEN, former CEO, Hanover Insurance

In the industrial age, the CEO sat on the top of the hierarchy and didn't have to listen to anybody.... In the information age, you have to listen to the ideas of people regardless of where they are in the organization.

　　―JOHN SCULLEY, former chairman, Apple Computer

The three basic ingredients of the capitalistic system: money, energy, and ideas.

　　―UNKNOWN

Our best ideas come from clerks and stockboys.

　　―SAM WALTON, founder, Wal-Mart

 *Improvement*

Whoever admits that he is too busy to improve his methods, has acknowledged himself to be at the end of his rope. And that is always the saddest predicament which anyone can get into.

　　―J. OGDEN ARMOUR, son of founder; former chairman, Armour & Co.

First ask yourself: What is the worst that can happen? Then prepare to accept it. Then proceed to improve on the worst.
    ━DALE CARNEGIE, author, *How to Win Friends and Influence People*

Improve constantly and forever the systems of production and service.
    ━W. EDWARDS DEMING, consultant and author, *Out of the Crisis*

When you aim for perfection, you discover it's a moving target.
    ━GEORGE FISHER, CEO, Kodak

When a business ceases to be creative, when it believes it has reached perfection and needs to do nothing but produce—no improvement, no development—it's done.
    ━HENRY FORD, founder, Ford Motor Company

At the end of every day of every year, two things remain unshakable, our constancy of purpose and our discontent with the immediate present.
    ━ROBERT C. GOIZUETA, former chairman and CEO, Coca-Cola

Measurement is the first step that leads to control and eventually to improvement. If you can't measure something, you can't understand it. If you can't understand it, you can't control it. If you can't control it, you can't improve it.
    ━H. JAMES HARRINGTON, consultant and author

The *kaizen* philosophy assumes that our way of life—be it our working life, our social life, or our home life—deserves to be constantly improved.
    ━MASAAKI IMAI, consultant and author, *Kaizen*

The ideas of control and improvement are often confused with one another. This is because quality control and quality improvement are inseparable.
    ━KAORU ISHIKAWA, founder, Union of Japanese Scientists and Engineers, president, Musashi Institute of Technology, and author, *Guide to Quality Control* and *What Is Total Quality Control?*

Good mistakes, those made with careful preparation and under-standing of the process in question, are valuable improvement tools. Good mistakes should be encouraged and rewarded as often and as thoroughly as possible.

—WILLIAM LAREAU, consultant and author, *American Samurai*

If you improve something by 1 percent each week, you will achieve a 14-fold improvement in 5 years. (Compound interest works wonders.

—JAMES MARTIN, chairman, James Martin & Co,. and author, *The Great Transition*

Excellent firms don't believe in excellence—only in constant improvement and constant change.

—TOM PETERS, consultant and author

Keep [this point] in mind. Improvement in a process should be a many splendored thing, involving all people and going on all the time as a way of life.

—HY PITT, consultant and author

Commit to CANI!—Constant And Never-ending Improvement

—ANTHONY ROBBINS, motivational speaker and author

⧼ Information Management ⧽

When you are drowning in numbers you need a system to separate the wheat from the chaff.

—ANTHONY ADAMS, VP, Campbell Soup Co.

There is a profound difference between information and meaning.

—WARREN BENNIS, founder and chair, Leadership Institute, University of Southern California

An individual without information cannot take responsibility; an individual who is given information cannot help but take responsibility.
— JAN CARLZON, former CEO, SAS, and author, *Moments of Truth*

Imagine a school with children that can read or write, but with teachers who cannot, and you have a metaphor of the Information Age in which we live.
— PETER COCHRANE, head of research, British Telecom

Knowledge is power, which is why people who had it in the past often tried to make a secret of it. In post-capitalism, power comes from transmitting information to make it productive, not from hiding it.
— PETER F. DRUCKER, consultant and renowned management author

One of the greatest pieces of economic wisdom is to know what you do not know.
— JOHN KENNETH GALBRAITH, economist

What I am describing here is a new level of information analysis that enables knowledge workers to turn passive data into active information—what M.I.T.'s Michael Dertouzos calls "information-as-a-verb."
— BILL GATES, founder and chairman, Microsoft

Individual contributors who gather and disseminate know-how and information should also be seen as middle managers, because they exert great power within the organization.
— ANDREW S. GROVE, former CEO, Intel Corp.

There is an especially efficient way to get information, much neglected by most managers. That is to visit a particular place in the company and observe what's going on there.
— ANDREW S. GROVE

Practically all large corporations insure their data bases against loss or damage or against their inability to gain access to them. Some day, on the corporate balance sheet, there will be an entry which reads, "Information," for in most cases, the information is more valuable than the hardware which processes it.

— GRACE MURRAY HOPPER, rear admiral U.S. Navy; developer of COBOL

I'd suggest you focus on information that tells you what you need to know under ordinary circumstances. That will give you an early warning when something extraordinary is going on.

— KENNETH F. IVERSON, CEO, Nucor

Never before has so much technology and information been available to mankind. Never before has mankind been so utterly confused. It's time for clarity.

— KPMG AD

In the industrial era information was like gold, providing those who had it with advantage and value. Today it is like milk. An ample supply which goes sour if not used within a short space of time.

— GERRY MCGOVERN, CEO, Nua

Data are most valuable at their point of origin. The value of data is directly related to their timeliness.

— LAWRENCE M. MILLER, president, Miller Consulting Group, and author, *Barbarians to Bureaucrats* and *From Management to Leadership*

We are drowning in information but starved for knowledge.

— JOHN NAISBITT, former executive with IBM and Eastman Kodak, and author, *Megatrends*, *Global Paradox*, and *High Tech/High Touch*

If you don't give people information, they'll make up something to fill the void.

— CARLA O'DELL, president, American Productivity & Quality Center

We can't do this on the basis of anecdotes. Get us the data.
— JOHN R. OPEL, former chairman, IBM

The information we have is not what we want.
The information we want is not what we need.
The information we need is not available.
— JOHN PEERS, president, Logical Machine Corporation

A man's judgment cannot be better than the information on which he has based it.
— ARTHUR HAYS SULZBERGER, former publisher, *The New York Times*

The tendency to hide unfavorable information often occurs in companies that are quick to reward success and equally quick to punish failure.
— ROBERT M. TOMASKO, principal, Temple, Barker & Sloane, Inc.

Information is power, and the gain you get from empowering your associates more than offsets the risk of informing your competitors
— SAM WALTON, founder, Wal-Mart

Innovation

Never kill an idea, just deflect it.
— 3M COMPANY SAYING

Innovation is the underpinning of perpetuating the organization.
— LAWRENCE BOSSIDY, chairman, Honeywell

Our company has, indeed, *stumbled* onto some of its new products. But never forget that you can only stumble if you're moving.
— RICHARD P. CARLETON, former CEO, 3M

The great discoveries are usually obvious.
  ━PHILIP CROSBY, consultant and author, *Quality Is Free*

The moral is that it is necessary to innovate, to predict needs of the customer, give him more. He that innovates and is lucky will take the market.
  ━W. EDWARDS DEMING, consultant and author, *Out of the Crisis*

We keep moving forward, opening new doors, and doing new things, because we're curious and curiosity keeps leading us down new paths.
  ━WALT DISNEY, founder, The Walt Disney Company

Every organization—not just businesses—needs one core competence: innovation. And every organization needs a way to record and appraise its innovative performance.
  ━PETER F. DRUCKER, consultant and renowned management author

The only big companies that succeed will be those that obsolete their own products before somebody else does.
  ━BILL GATES, founder and chairman, Microsoft

Innovation means that people are working together. It means that there's an information flow from within the organization and from without. It means that there's an environment that honors ideas, that doesn't punish people for taking risks, and that makes it easy for people to interact with each other.
  ━GINA IMPERATO, founder, Innovation Network

Innovation takes an unreasonable man.
  ━JONATHAN IVE, VP of product design, Apple Computers

By far the greatest flow of newness is not innovation at all. Rather, it is imitation.
  ━THEODORE LEVITT, former editor, *Harvard Business Review,* and professor emeritus of business administration, Harvard University

Creativity is thinking up new things. Innovation is doing new things.

— THEODORE LEVITT, former editor, *Harvard Business Review,* and professor emeritus of business administration, Harvard University

Invention is a flower. Innovation is a weed.

— BOB METCALFE, inventor, Ethernet, founder, 3COM, and VP, technology, International Data Group

Creative craziness is what drives innovation. And being creatively crazy means saying, "I don't care what the system wants. I don't care what the system allows. You made me the principal—or CEO—of this place. Now step back."

— LORRAINE MONROE, former principal, Frederick Douglass Intermediate School in New York City, director, School Leadership Academy at the Center for Educational Innovation, and author, *Nothing's Impossible: Leadership Lessons from Inside and Outside the Classroom*

Innovation comes only from readily and seamlessly sharing information rather than hoarding it.

— TOM PETERS, consultant and author

One of the most interesting things about inventions is that when it's all worked out, it looks obvious, but for some strange reason was not obvious enough to have been done before.

— JACK RABINOW, founder, Rabinow Engineering and RABCO Company, and inventor (more than 230 patents)

Good ideas and innovations must be driven into existence by courageous patience.

— HYMAN RICKOVER, admiral and founder of the nuclear navy

It requires a better type of mind to seek out and to support or to create the new than to follow the worn paths of accepting success.

— JOHN D. ROCKEFELLER, founder, Standard Oil

The people who get into trouble in our company are those who carry around the anchor of the past.

— JACK WELCH, chairman and CEO, General Electric

 *Integrity*

Preserve your integrity. It is more precious than diamonds or rubies.

— P.T. BARNUM, circus owner

Do not look for approval except for the consciousness of doing your best.

— BERNARD BARUCH, American financier and presidential advisor

Be daring, be different, be impractical, be anything that will assert integrity of purpose and imaginative vision against the play-it-safers, the creatures of the commonplace, the slaves of the ordinary.

— SIR CECIL BEATON, photographer and stage designer

Somebody once said that in looking for people to hire, you look for three qualities: integrity, intelligence, and energy. And if they don't have the first, the other two will kill you.

— WARREN BUFFET, CEO, Berkshire Hathaway

It takes 20 years to build a reputation and five minutes to ruin it. If you think about that, you'll do things differently.

— WARREN BUFFET

No amount of ability is of the slightest avail without honor.

— ANDREW CARNEGIE, founder, U.S. Steel

Just being honest is not enough. The essential ingredient is executive integrity.

— PHILIP CROSBY, consultant and author, *Quality Is Free*

I am proud of the fact that I never invented weapons to kill.
—THOMAS A. EDISON, **American inventor**

When young, you're shocked by the number of people who have feet of clay. Older, you're surprised by the number of people who don't.
—MALCOLM FORBES, **former publisher,** *Forbes* **magazine**

If humanity does not opt for integrity we are through completely. It is absolutely touch and go. Each one of us could make the difference.
—R. BUCKMINSTER FULLER, **inventor and idea provocateur**

Integrity is the essence of everything successful.
—R. BUCKMINSTER FULLER

Hire and promote first on the basis of integrity; second, motivation; third, capacity; fourth, understanding; fifth, knowledge; and last and least, experience.
—DEE HOCK, **founder and CEO emeritus, VISA USA and VISA International**

In matters of principle, stand like a rock; in matters of taste, swim with the current.
—THOMAS JEFFERSON, **U.S. President**

If you believe in unlimited quality and act in all your business dealings with total integrity, the rest will take care of itself.
—FRANK PERDUE, **founder, Perdue Farms**

I believe in the sacredness of a promise, that a man's word should be as good as his bond; that character—not wealth or power or position—is of supreme worth
—JOHN D. ROCKEFELLER, JR., **U.S. oil magnate and philanthropist**

Have the courage to say no. Have the courage to face the truth. Do the right thing because it is right. These are the magic keys to living your life with integrity.
—W. CLEMENT STONE, **author,** *Think and Grow Rich*

There is a time when integrity should take the rudder from team loyalty.

━THOMAS J. WATSON, JR., son of founder and former chairman, IBM

 *Intelligence*

Be smart, be intelligent and be informed.

━TONY ALLESSANDRA, author, *People Smarts,* and coauthor, *The Platinum Rule*

The most important thing in life is not simply to capitalize on your gains. Any fool can do that. The important thing is to profit from your losses. That requires intelligence and makes the difference between a man of sense and a fool.

━DALE CARNEGIE, author, *How to Win Friends and Influence People*

When your views on the world and your intellect are being challenged and you begin to feel uncomfortable because of a contradiction you've detected that is threatening your current model of the world or some aspect of it, pay attention. You are about to learn something. This discomfort and intellectual conflict is when learning is taking place.

━WILLIAM H. DRURY, director of research and education, Massachusetts Audubon Society, and member, President's Science Advisory Committees (Kennedy and Nixon), and professor of evolutionary biology, Harvard University and College of the Atlantic

[Smart] is an elusive concept. There's a certain sharpness, an ability to absorb new facts, to ask an insightful question, or relate to domains that may not seem connected at first, a certain creativity that allows people to be effective.

━BILL GATES, founder and chairman, Microsoft

The brain is a mass of cranial nerve tissue, most of it in mint condition.

— ROBERT HALF, founder, Robert Half International

A man must have a certain amount of intelligent ignorance to get anywhere.

— CHARLES F. KETTERING, president, General Motors Research Corp.,   and cofounder, Sloan-Kettering Institute for Cancer Research

Intelligence is the effort to do the best you can at your particulate job; the quality that gives dignity to that job, whether it happens to be scrubbing a floor or running a corporation.

— JAMES C. PENNEY, founder, J.C. Penney stores

Any intelligent fool can make things bigger, more complex, and more violent. It takes a touch of genius—and a lot of courage—to move in the opposite direction.

— E.F. SCHUMACHER, author, *Small Is Beautiful*

The quest quotient has always excited me more than the intelligence quotient.

— EUGENE WILSON, dean of admissions, Amherst, and director and executive committee member, College Entrance Examination Board and National Merit Selection Committee

I use not only all the brains I have, but all I can borrow.

— WOODROW WILSON, U.S. President

Interdependence

The influence of each human on others in this life is a kind of immortality.

➤ JOHN QUINCY ADAMS, U.S. President

We didn't all come over on the same ship, but we're all in the same boat.

➤ BERNARD BARUCH, American financier and presidential advisor

A system is a network of interdependent components that work together to try to accomplish the aim of the system. A system must have an aim. Without an aim, there is no system. ... A system must be managed. The secret is cooperation between components toward the aim of the organization.

➤ W. EDWARDS DEMING, consultant and author, *Out of the Crisis*

What we need to do is learn to work in the system, by which I mean that everybody, every team, every platform, every division, every component is there not for individual competitive profit or recognition, but for contribution to the system as a whole on a win-win basis.

➤ W. EDWARDS DEMING

In the ethics of interdependence there are only obligations, and all obligations are mutual obligations. Harmony and trust—that is, interdependence—require that each side be obligated to provide what the other side needs to achieve its goals and to fulfill itself.

➤ PETER F. DRUCKER, consultant and renowned management author

You will find men who want to be carried on the shoulders of others, who think that the world owes them a living. They don't seem to see that we must all lift together and pull together.

➤ HENRY FORD, founder, Ford Motor Company

All humanity is one undivided and indivisible family, and each one of us is responsible for the misdeeds of all the others.

━MOHANDAS K. GHANDI, **leader, Indian independence movement**

The organization is just a vehicle for human cooperation.

━FRANCIS GOUILLART (senior VP) AND JAMES KELLY, (cochairman), **Gemini Consulting, and coauthors,** *Transforming the Organization*

I think of my work in the context of a global cocktail party. Lots of people are standing around a ballroom. Some are at the periphery, just holding their drinks and watching life go by. Others are on the dance floor, in groups of two or three. My job is to work the crowd—because each of these people may hold a clue to the reason for my existence.

━BRIAN KOVAL, **manager, Ryder Carrier Management**

A company is a multidimensional system capable of growth, expansion, and self-regulation. It is, therefore, not a thing but a set of interacting forces.

━ALBERT LOW, **author,** *Zen and Creative Management*

Life is like a cob web, not an organization chart.

━H. ROSS PEROT, **founder, EDS and Perot Systems**

If we are to compete effectively in today's world, we must begin to celebrate collective entrepreneurship, endeavors in which the whole of the effort is greater than the sum of the individual contributions. We need to honor our teams more, our aggressive leaders and maverick geniuses less.

━ROBERT REICH, **former Secretary of Labor, Clinton Administration**

The average American salesman keeps 33 men and women at work—33 people producing the product he sell—and is responsible for the livelihood of 130 people.

━ROBERT A. WHITNEY, **president, New York Stock Exchange**

When you think about it, *debt* is a way of measuring just how inter-dependent we all are.

—JOHN WOODS, president, CWL Publishing Enterprises

The truth is that *everything* that happens impacts everything else. Everything is interconnected, and as such, everything that is happening in your consumer's world matters to you.

—SERGIO ZYMAN, chief marketing officer, Coca-Cola

Knowledge Management

There is much talk about the high importance of "knowledge management" and "intellectual capital" in the unorganized world in which we work with our heads and not with our hands. In the unorganized world, the only property that matters is intellectual property, the only matter that matters is brain matter.

—SIMON BUCKINGHAM, founder, Unorganization

Over the years, man has taught himself to hoard knowledge to achieve power. Today, we have to reverse that tendency. Today, the most powerful individuals will be those who become a source of knowledge by sharing what they have—of what they can get their hands on—with others.

—ROBERT BUCKMAN, president, Buckman Labs

Knowledge derives from minds at work.

—THOMAS H. DAVENPORT AND LAURENCE PRUSAK, authors, *Working Knowledge*

Successful knowledge transfer involves neither computers nor documents but rather interactions between people.

—THOMAS H. DAVENPORT, consultant and coauthor, *Working Knowledge*

We can no longer compete on the cost of labor with countries like China. What we have to leverage is our know-how.
> ➤CARLO DE BENEDETTI, CEO, Olivetti

The increase in productivity has been caused primarily by the replacement of labor by planning, brawn by brain, sweat by knowledge.
> ➤PETER F. DRUCKER, consultant and renowned management author

The very essence of human progress is applying new knowledge in new ways, continuously making the old way of doing things obsolete.
> ➤FRANCIS GOUILLART (senior VP) AND JAMES KELLY, (cochairman), Gemini Consulting, and coauthors, *Transforming the Organization*

Forget land, buildings, or machines—the real source of wealth today is intelligence, applied intelligence. We talk glibly of "intellectual property" without taking on board what it really means. It isn't just patent rights and brand names; it is the brains of the place.
> ➤CHARLES HANDY, cofounder, London Business School and author, *Understanding Organizations* and *Beyond Certainty: The Changing Worlds of Organizations*

It is safe to assume that knowledge as a concept is far from manageable, even at its most concrete level, of say, knowledge as an asset—we can barely measure it, and yet we assume that we can apply "management" techniques to it. To cope with this, I have opted to replace the term with *knowledge orchestration*.
> ➤RONEN HIRSCH, Tikal Software Industries Ltd.

We are failing to get value out of our businesses if we don't spend attention and resources on getting knowledge and best practices around the company.
> ➤STEPHEN HUGGINS, chief knowledge officer and VP, strategic planning, B.F. Goodrich

Don't educate, focus on relentlessly reducing knowledge-sharing's transaction costs instead.
> ➤JOSEPH J. KATZMAN, senior management consultant, KPMG Electronic Markets

Knowledge is what we get when an observer, preferably a scientifically trained observer, provides us with a copy of reality that we can all recognize.

—CHRISTOPHER LASCH, historian, social critic, and author, *Haven in a Heartless World*, *The Culture of Narcissism*, and *The Revolt of the Elites*

One of the hazards of the mechanical as opposed to biological view of organizations is that in the name of eliminating redundancy, it tends to strip out people with intangible roles that actually create value from intangible assets. Today's organizations need communicator bees as well as worker bees.

—THOMAS STEWART, member, board of editors, *Fortune* magazine, and author, *Intellectual Capital: The New Wealth of Organizations*

Knowledge is the most democratic source of power.

—ALVIN TOFFLER, author, *Future Shock!*

Labor Relations

Had the employers of the past generation dealt fairly with men, there would have been no trade unions.

—STANLEY BALDWIN, former Prime Minister, Great Britain

Leave my factories but take away my people and soon grass will grow on my factory floors. Take my factories, but leave my people, and soon we will have new and better plants.

—ANDREW CARNEGIE, founder, U.S. Steel

Labor is the capital of our working man.

—GROVER CLEVELAND, U.S. President

Industry must manage to keep wages high and prices low. Otherwise it will limit the number of its customers. One's own employees should be one's best customers.

—HENRY FORD, founder, Ford Motor Company

Show me the country in which there are no strikes and I'll show you that country in which there is no liberty.

—SAMUEL GOMPERS, early labor leader

Let every employer get this into his mind: Production resulting from long hours worked unwillingly cannot but be less satisfactory than production from shorter hours worked willingly.

—CARTER GOODRICH, historian and editor, *The Government and the Economy, 1783-1861*

Labor disgraces no man; unfortunately you occasionally find men disgrace labor.

—ULYSSES S. GRANT, U.S. President

I want workers to go home at night and say, "I built that car."

—PEHR G. GYLLENHAMMAR, chairman of the board, MC European Capital S.A., former CEO, AB Volvo

The interesting prospect about an economy with fewer workers is that they will choose where they will work. Some will force companies to offer much higher salaries and wages. Others will challenge their companies to manage them well, both to increase production and to keep them from leaving.

—BILL HUNTER, president, Hunter Associates

The cement in our whole democracy today is the worker who makes $15 an hour. He's the guy who will buy a house and a car and a refrigerator. He's the oil in the engine.

—LEE IACOCCA, former chairman, Chrysler Corp.

Anybody who has any doubt about the ingenuity or the resource-fulness of a plumber never got a bill from one.

— GEORGE MEANY, former president, AFL-CIO

We try for an interchange of ideas and principles—something more than a boss-employee relationship—in order to involve the worker.

— JOHN MOLLICA, assistant director for labor relations, General Motors

Employers generally get the kind of labor relations they ask for.

— PHILIP MURRAY, director, CIO

I believe in the dignity of labor, whether with head or hand; that the world owes no man a living but that it owes every man an opportunity to make a living.

— JOHN D. ROCKEFELLER, JR., U.S. oil magnate and philanthropist

It is one of the characteristics of a free and democratic nation that it have free and independent labor unions.

— FRANKLIN D. ROOSEVELT, U.S. PRESIDENT

Changes are impossible to bring off when managers and unions are adversaries.

— DEAN M. RUWE, senior VP, Copeland Corporation

Most labor-management problems occur because we forget we are all in business to serve customers.

— RICHARD TEERLINK, former CEO, Harley-Davidson

Leadership

The key to successful leadership today is influence, not authority.
  ━KENNETH BLANCHARD, **consultant and author**

A leader is a dealer in hope.
  ━NAPOLEON BONAPARTE, **former emperor of France**

Ineffective leaders often act on the advice and counsel of the last person they talked to.
  ━WARREN G. BENNIS, **founder and chair, Leadership Institute, University of Southern California**

The most dangerous leadership myth is that leaders are born—that there is a genetic factor to leadership. This myth asserts that people simply either have certain charismatic qualities or not. That's nonsense; in fact, the opposite is true. Leaders are made rather than born.
  ━WARREN G. BENNIS

A leader takes people where they want to go. A great leader takes people where they don't necessarily want to go but ought to be.
  ━ROSALYNN CARTER, **former First Lady**

If you're a high-profile charismatic leader, fine. But if you're not, then that's fine, too, for you're in good company right along with those that built companies like 3M, P&G, Sony, Boeing, HP, and Merck. Not a bad crowd.
  ━JAMES C. COLLINS AND JERRY I. PORRAS, **authors, *Built to Last***

Management works *in* the system; Leadership works *on* the system.
  ━STEPHEN COVEY, **consultant and author, *The 7 Habits of Highly Effective People***

I know a leader when I have followed one.

    —JOHN COWAN, author, *Small Decencies*

In a day when so much energy seems to be spent on maintenance and manuals, on bureaucracy and meaningless quantification, to be a leader is to enjoy special privileges of complexity, of ambiguity, of diversity.

    —MAX DEPREE, former CEO, Herman Miller, Inc., and author, *Leadership Jazz*

Lincoln chose his general for his tested ability to win battles and not for his sobriety, that is, for the absence of a weakness.

    —PETER F. DRUCKER, consultant and renowned management author

Leadership is the art of getting someone else to do something you want done because he wants to do it.

    —DWIGHT D. EISENHOWER, U.S. President

A leader's skill is best rated not by how smoothly things run while you're there, but how well they go after you have left.

    —SALLY HELGESEN, author, *The Female Advantage: Women's Ways of Leadership*

We must remember that knowledge workers keep their tool kits in their heads. We must learn to lead people, not contain them. We must learn to listen.

    —FRANCES HESSELBEIN, executive director, Girl Scouts USA

Make a careful list of all things done to you that you abhorred. Don't do them to others, ever. Make another list of things done for you that you loved. Do them for others, always.

    —DEE HOCK, founder and CEO emeritus, VISA USA and VISA International

Leadership has a harder job to do than just choose sides. It must bring sides together.

    —JESSE JACKSON, civil rights leader

Leadership is discovering the company's destiny and having the courage to follow it.

— JOE JAWORSKI, **head, Royal Dutch Shell scenario planning group, and author,** *Synchronicity: The Inner Path of Leadership*

The best leaders will be those who listen to their people to figure out where they should be going.

— JACK KAHL, **CEO and chairman, Manco, Inc.**

Leaders can't succeed if they care more about how people feel than how they perform.

— MARILYN MOATS KENNEDY, **managing partner, Career Strategies**

The most important part of being a leader is maintaining the desire to keep on learning. That means learning about yourself, about your peers, and about the people you serve.

— BRIAN KOVAL, **manager, Ryder Carrier Management**

Leadership is a matter of having people look at you and gain confidence, seeing how you react. If you're in control, they're in control.

— TOM LANDRY, **former coach, Dallas Cowboys**

Leaders aren't born, they are made. And they are made just like anything else, through hard work. And that's the price we'll have to pay to achieve that goal, or any goal.

— VINCE LOMBARDI, **legendary coach, Green Bay Packers**

A good leader is a person who takes a little more than his share of the blame and a little less than his share of the credit.

— JOHN C. MAXWELL, **minister and author,** *Developing the Leader Within You, Developing the Leaders Around You*, **and** *21 Irrefutable Laws of Leadership*

I start with the premise that the function of leadership is to produce more leaders, not more followers.

— RALPH NADER, **consumer advocate**

Leadership appears to be the art of getting others to want to do something you are convinced should be done.

→VANCE PACKARD, author, *The Hidden Persuaders* and *The Pyramid Climbers*

There are all kinds of ways to learn to be a leader. The foolish way is to think that there is a type of ideal leader, and to try to become that. The smart way is to learn how to be a better Sasha or Natalie or Bruce, and then to find out where and how you can be effective in making changes in the world.

→BRUCE L. PAYNE, director, Leadership and the Arts, Duke University

In order simply to survive in life, let alone be a leader, you must learn to take responsibility for the way things affect you. At the same time, you must learn to bend with the wind of forces too great for your control.

→JIM ROHN, entrepreneur and author, 7 *Strategies for Wealth and Happiness*

A Leader must possess credibility, imagination, enthusiasm, vision, foresight, a sense of timing, a passion for excellence and be willing to share.

→WILLIAM ROSENBERG, founder, Dunkin' Donuts

Leadership is a potent combination of strategy and character. But if you must be without one, be without the strategy.

→H. NORMAN SCHWARZKOPF, general and commander, Gulf War

Leaders in learning organizations are responsible for building organizations where people are continually expanding their capabilities to share their future—that is, leaders are responsible for learning.

→PETER SENGE, consultant, speaker, and author, *The Fifth Discipline*

The critical roles of leaders: designer, teacher, and steward.

→PETER SENGE

Leaders get out in front and stay there by raising the standards by which they judge themselves—and by which they are willing to be judged.

  ⟵FREDRICK SMITH, **founder and CEO, Federal Express**

Leadership derives naturally from a commitment to service. You know that you're practicing servant leadership if your followers become wiser, healthier, more autonomous—and more likely to become servant leaders themselves.

  ⟵JIM STUART, **cofounder, The Leadership Circle**

The most important job for a leader who wants to win in the 21st century is to create more leaders, at more levels of your company, than the competition.

  ⟵NOEL TICHY, **director, Global Leadership Program, University of Michigan Business School**

A leader is not an administrator who loves to run others, but someone who carries water for his people so they can get on with their jobs.

  ⟵ROBERT TOWNSEND, **former CEO, Avis Rent-a-Car, and author,** *Up the Organization*

If you look at what leaders do, in the end if they leave a legacy, then they've done something, and if they don't, then it's just footprints in the sand.

  ⟵JOHN TRANI, **chairman and CEO, The Stanley Works**

The first principle of leadership is authenticity: "Watch what I do, not what I say."

  ⟵HATIM TYABJI, **president and CEO, Verifone Inc.**

Good business leaders create a vision, articulate the vision, passionately own the vision, and relentlessly drive it to completion.

  ⟵JACK WELCH, **chairman and CEO, General Electric**

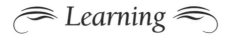 Learning

History is the sum total of things that could have been avoided.

—KONRAD ADENAUER, former Chancellor, Germany

Success in the marketplace increasingly depends on learning, yet most people don't know how to learn. What's more, those members of the organization that many assume to be the best at learning are, in fact, not very good at it.

—CHRIS ARGYRIS, professor, Harvard Business School

Education is learning what you didn't even know you didn't know.

DANIEL BOORSTIN, historian and former head, Library of Congress

The important thing about science is not so much to obtain new facts as to discover new ways of thinking about them.

—WILLIAM BRAGG, British scientist and winner of the Nobel Prize for Physics (1915)

Making a wrong decision is understandable. Refusing to search continually for learning is not.

—PHILIP CROSBY, consultant and author, *Quality Is Free*

The ability to learn faster than your competitors may be the only sustainable competitive advantage.

—ARIE P. DE GEUS, former coordinator, group planning, Royal Dutch/Shell, and senior lecturer, London Business School

Learning is not compulsory, but neither is survival.

—W. EDWARDS DEMING, consultant and author, *Out of the Crisis*

Dare to be naive.

—R. BUCKMINSTER FULLER, inventor and idea provocateur

Learning ... happens all through life unless we block it. Organizations therefore need, consciously, to beome learning organizations, places where change is an opportunity, where people grow while they work.

— CHARLES HANDY, cofounder, London Business School and author, *Understanding Organizations* and *Beyond Certainty: The Changing Worlds of Organizations*

Liberty without learning is always in peril, and learning without liberty is always in vain.

— JOHN F. KENNEDY, U.S. President

The young man who has the combination of the learning of books with the learning which comes of doing things need not worry about getting along in the world today, or at any time.

— WILLIAM S. KNUDSEN, former president, General Motors

Lessons are usually where you look for them. You can learn something from anyone.

— BRIAN KOVAL, manager, Ryder Carrier Management

Are you green and growing or ripe and rotting?

— RAY KROC, founder, McDonald's

Progress consists largely of learning to apply laws and truths that have always existed.

— JOHN ALLAN MAY, author, *Complete Book of Golf: A Guide to Equipment, Techniques, and Courses*

Give me a fruitful error any time, full of seeds, bursting with its own corrections. You can keep your sterile truth for yourself.

— VILFREDO PARETO, mathematician and inventor of the Pareto (80-20) Principle

The key work in any business, of course, is *learning*. Walton and Roddick learned from their early pratfalls, small and large, and made adjustment after adjustment after adjustment...
> —Tom Peters, consultant and author

Prosperity belongs to those who learn new things the fastest.
> —Paul Zane Pilzer, economic advisor to presidents Reagan and Bush, and author, *Unlimited Wealth* and *God Wants You to Be Rich*

The secret of success is learning how to use pain and pleasure instead of having pain and pleasure use you. If you do that, you're in control of your life. If you don't, life controls you.
> —Anthony Robbins, motivational speaker and author

We in top management are responsible for creating an operating environment that can allow continual learning.
> —Richard Teerlink, former CEO, Harley-Davidson

The illiterate of the 21st century will not be those who cannot read and write, but those who cannot learn, unlearn, and relearn.
> —Alvin Toffler, author, *Future Shock!*

There's no age here to retire. As long as you're interested in learning and can transfer knowledge, you're a good source of intellectual capital.
> —Rene Villarreal, CEO, PIPSA

An organization's ability to learn, and translate that learning into action rapidly, is the ultimate competitive business advantage.
> —Jack Welch, chairman and CEO, General Electric

It's not whether we have learned from history—we have—but our awareness of what we have learned.
> —John Woods, president, CWL Publishing Enterprises

 Life Balance

Nobody should work all the time. Everyone should have some leisure, but I believe the early morning hours are best for this—the five or six hours when you're asleep.

—GEORGE ALLEN, former football coach, Washington Redskins

Just when I've convinced myself that what I have is more than plenty, the phone rings, and someone offers me something I can't resist. But then I ask an important question: How thin can I spread myself before I'm no longer "there"?

—JOHN PERRY BARLOW, cofounder, Electronic Frontier Foundation

Balance is an illusion—and to have it as a goal is self-defeating. Instead, take advantage of whatever trade-offs you can make.

—MELINDA BROWN, VP, Lotus Development Corporation

I don't know how much faster and harder we can all go. There has to be a breaking point. Maybe then we'll be able to slow down and accept a certain level of tedium and repetition. We might have fewer toys, but we'd be able to simplify our world and to enjoy life.

—MELINDA BROWN

Put yourself in a position where you're making choices about your life, rather than letting other people make those choices for you. That's what balance is all about.

—LIZ DOLAN, president, Dolan St. Clair Inc.

I can tell that I've hit the wall at work and that I need to recalibrate my life, when I can no longer empathize with others, when I'm focused only on results, when I ignore other people's goals, and when I become frustrated with life's interruptions. Or when my daughter has to tell me, "It'll be all right, Kirby."

—KIRBY DYESS, VP and director of new product development, Intel Corporation

There is more to life than increasing its speed.

> ━MOHANDAS K. GANDHI, leader, Indian independence movement

Put your emotional life in order.... It's a great help in climbing toward the higher rungs of the career ladder, to be happy in life, rather than find yourself mired in emotional crisis. It's hard enough to succeed without taking on personal problems that sap your energy and divert your attention.

> ━MICHAEL KORDA, author, *Success* and *Power! How to Use It, How to Get It*

When I hear a man talk about how hard he works, and how he hasn't taken a vacation in five years, and how seldom he sees his family, I am certain that this man will not succeed in the creative aspects of business ... and most of the important things that have to be done are the result of creative acts.

> ━HERMAN C. KRANNERT, founder, Inland Container Corporation

When it comes to progress, I am a work in progress.

> ━DAWN GOULD LEPORE, executive VP and chief information officer, Charles Schwab Corporation

I often hear people proudly claim that they work 100-hour weeks. The first thing I think is how can a person really be effective for 100 hours?

> ━DAVID LUNSFORD, director of advanced technology, Dell Computer

There are people at Sprint who work from sunup to well past sundown: they become their jobs. They might make it to middle management, but then they get stuck. They can't lift their heads above the trenches. They're horrible managers because they expect the whole world to behave and work as they do.

> ━PATTI MANUEL, president and COO, long-distance division, Sprint

A friendship founded on business is a good deal better than a business founded on friendship.

　—JOHN D. ROCKEFELLER, founder, Standard Oil

I can think of nothing less pleasurable than a life devoted to pleasure.

　—JOHN D. ROCKEFELLER, JR., U.S. oil magnate and philanthropist

People who cannot find time for recreation are obliged sooner or later to find time for illness.

　—JOHN WANAMAKER, founder, Wanamaker Department Stores

Listening

Most men talk too much. Much of my success has been due to keeping my mouth shut.

　—J. OGDEN ARMOUR, president, Armour Meat Packing Co.

Listen long enough and the person will generally come up with an adequate solution.

　—MARY KAY ASH, founder, Mary Kay Cosmetics

One often hears the remark, "He talks too much," but when did anyone last hear the criticism, "He listens too much"?

　—NORMAN AUGUSTINE, CEO, Lockheed Martin

An inability to stay quiet is one of the conspicuous failings of mankind.

　—WALTER BAGEHOT, founding editor, *The Economist*

The habit of common and continuous speech is a symptom of mental deficiency. It proceeds from not knowing what is going on in other people's minds.

— WALTER BAGEHOT, founding editor, *The Economist*

Most of the successful people I've known are the ones who do more listening than talking.

— BERNARD BARUCH, American financier and presidential advisor

Listening, not imitation, may be the sincerest form of flattery.

— JOYCE BROTHERS, author and psychologist

You can make more friends in two months by becoming genuinely interested in other people than you can in two years by trying to get other people interested in you.

— DALE CARNEGIE, author, *How to Win Friends and Influence People*

My greatest strength as a consultant is to be ignorant and ask a few questions.

— PETER F. DRUCKER, consultant and renowned management author

Coaches have to watch for what they don't want to see and listen to what they don't want to hear.

— JOHN MADDEN, former football coach and sports broadcaster

Listen to everyone in your company, and figure out ways to get them talking. The folks on the front line—the ones who actually talk to customers—are the only ones who really know what's going on out there. You'd better find out what they know.

— SAM WALTON, founder, Wal-Mart

One important reason to listen is that it teaches others to listen to you.

— JOHN WOODS, president, CWL Publishing Enterprises

Listening helps you bring out of yourself the things you didn't know were there.

—JOHN WOODS, **president, CWL Publishing Enterprises**

Management

Management skills are only part of what it takes.... Managers must also be corporate *warriors* or *leaders*. These unique individuals are the problem identifiers. They possess a strong sense of vision; view fire fighting as an opportunity to do things differently and smarter; and are business strategists who help identify key corporate growth issues.

—JOHN W. ALDRIDGE, **president, Aldridge Associates**

For a manager to be perceived as a positive manager, he needs a four to one positive to negative contact ratio.

—KENNETH BLANCHARD, **consultant and author**

Look at management as a function, not a class. If you go into the role thinking that management is a class, you'll be sorely disappointed when you find that people rebel against you.

—MIKE BUSCH, **cofounder and editor-in-chief, AVweb**

The basic cause of sickness in American industry and resulting unemployment is failure of top management to manage.

—W. EDWARDS DEMING, **consultant and author,** *Out of the Crisis*

"Management" means, in the last analysis, the substitution of thought for brawn and muscle, of knowledge for folkways and superstition, and of cooperation for force. It means the substitution of responsibility for obedience to rank, and of authority of performance for authority of rank.

—PETER F. DRUCKER, **consultant and renowned management author**

So much of what we call management consists in making it difficult for people to work.

— PETER F. DRUCKER, consultant and renowned management author

Where are you likely to find people with the least diversity of experience, the largest investment in the past, and the greatest reverence for industry dogma? At the top.

— GARY HAMEL, consultant and author

It is most important for me to be personally involved in seeing the vision and direction of the company and then being able to communicate it so our people buy into it. My second most important role is the development and placement of people in the global management team and then my personal involvement in our investments, our growth, and our acquisitions.

— GERALD B. JOHANNSON, CEO, Haworth Inc.

The man who gets the most satisfactory results is not always the man with the most brilliant single mind, but rather the man who can best coordinate the brains and talents of his associates.

— W. ALTON JONES, chairman, Cities Service Company (CITGO), and author, *The Cities Service Story*

The key to surviving in this age of global competition is to see how well we can apply the power of the individual to our organization as we acquire and nurture talent.

— TAKASHI KAMIO, managing director, Toyota Motor Corporation

If you're the chief executive officer you get more blame than you deserve, and you also get more credit than you deserve. If you want one, you've got to accept the other too.

— K.T. KELLER, president (1935-1950) and chairman (1950-1956), Chrysler Corporation

The key question for top management is what are your assumptions (implicit as well as explicit) about the most effective way to manage people. The assumptions management holds about controlling its human resources determine the whole character of the enterprise.

—DOUGLAS McGREGOR, **author and creator of "Theory X" and "Theory Y"**

As you get better at your work, your organization gets better at *its* work: the people who do the frontline work improve. And as you transform your company, you transform yourself.

—LORRAINE MONROE, **former principal, Frederick Douglass Intermediate School in New York City, director, School Leadership Academy at the Center for Educational Innovation, and author,** *Nothing's Impossible: Leadership Lessons from Inside and Outside the Classroom*

Good management consists in showing average people how to do the work of superior people.

—JOHN D. ROCKEFELLER, **founder, Standard Oil**

Nobody should be chief executive of anything for more than five or six years. By then he's stale, bored, and utterly dependent on his own clichés—though they may have been revolutionary ideas when he first brought them to the office.

—ROBERT TOWNSEND, **former CEO, Avis Rent-a-Car, and author,** *Up the Organization*

Top management (the board of directors) is supposed to be a tree full of owls—hooting when management heads into the wrong part of the forest. I'm still unpersuaded that they even know where the forest is.

—ROBERT TOWNSEND

The primary purpose of good corporation management is to keep a company in business indefinitely.

— CHARLES E. WILSON, **former CEO, General Motors, and Secretary of Defense in the Eisenhower administration**

Robot executives who cling to this-is-the-way-it's-always-been-done conformity are not only stifling their own careers but are precipitating a case of hardening of the arteries throughout U.S. industry.

— LOUIS WOLFSON, **financier**

 *Managing*

Treat employees like partners, and they act like partners.

— FRED ALLEN, **chairman, Pitney-Bowes Co.**

Try as far as possible to pass on information rather than your conclusions. Your conclusions, if they are right, are part of your competitive advantage. If they are wrong and you pass them on, they may come back to haunt you.

— MARY ANN ALLISON, **principal, The Allison Group, LLC**

There are two things people want more than sex and money— recognition and praise.

— MARY KAY ASH, **founder, Mary Kay Cosmetics**

Participative management is, simply stated, involving the right people at the right time in the decision process.

— WAYNE BARLOW, **administrator, Federal Aviation Agency**

Anymore, managing my people is like herding cats. Cats, of course, won't allow themselves to be herded.

—WARREN BENNIS, **founder and chair, Leadership Institute, University of Southern California**

Boss your boss just as soon as you can; try it on early. There is nothing he will like so well if he is the right kind of boss; if he is not, he is not the man for you to remain with.

—ANDREW CARNEGIE, **founder, U.S. Steel**

[Managing:] Giving every employee the means, motivation, and opportunity to do their jobs.

—TOM CORCORAN, **VP, IBM**

Instead of setting numerical quotas, management should work on improvement of the process.

—W. EDWARDS DEMING, **consultant and author,** *Out of the Crisis*

Effective executives never ask, "How does he get along with me?" Their question is "What does he contribute?"

—PETER F. DRUCKER, **consultant and renowned management author**

There is nothing so useless as doing efficiently that which should not be done at all.

—PETER F. DRUCKER

As a leader, I find that the best thing I can do for people who work with me is to ask them what's important to them—and then to give them permission to get away from work so that they can do it.

—KIRBY DYESS, **VP and director, new product development, Intel Corporation**

Delegating work works, provided the one delegating works, too.

—ROBERT HALF, **founder, Robert Half International**

Those who try to paint a management picture "by the numbers" will always be amateurs.

→ JAMES L. HAYES, former president, American Management Association

Whenever decisions are made strictly on the basis of bottom-line arithmetic, human beings get crunched along with the numbers.

→ THOMAS R. HORTON, president and CEO, American Management Association

In the end, all business operations can be reduced to three words: people, product, and profits. People come first.

→ LEE IACOCCA, former chairman, Chrysler Corp.

When Alexander the Great visited Diogenes he asked whether he could do anything for the famous teacher. And Diogenes just simply said, "Just stay out of my light."

→ ALEXANDER KROLL, CEO, Young and Rubicam

The secret to winning is constant, consistent management.

→ TOM LANDRY. former football coach, Dallas Cowboys

Persuasion, kind, unassuming persuasion, should be adopted to influence the conduct of men. The opposite course would be a reversal of human nature, which is God's decree and can never be reversed.

→ ABRAHAM LINCOLN, U.S. President

Between the two extremes of guesswork and formula there is a middle ground on which most managers operate. Here they recognize occasions that demand situational leadership—appropriately autocratic or laissez-faire—and other occasions that permit the integration of human resources with conscious renewal processes. Organizational renewal can live quite comfortably in this middle ground.

→ GORDON L. LIPPITT, former professor, School of Government and Business Administration, George Washington University, founder, International Consultants Foundation, and author, *The Consulting Process in Action*

I try to create an environment in which people know that it's okay to not be a workaholic—in which they get ahead because of their contribution, not because of the number of hours they clock.
> ←PATTI MANUEL, president and COO, long-distance division, Sprint

The more high-tech around us, the more the need for human touch.
> ←JOHN NAISBITT, former executive with IBM and Eastman Kodak, and author, *Megatrends*, *Global Paradox*, and *High Tech/High Touch*

People think the president has to be the main organizer. No, the president is the main disorganizer. Everybody *manages* quite well; whenever anything goes wrong, they take immediate action to make sure nothing'll go wrong again. The problem is, nothing new will ever happen, either.
> ←HARRY QUADRACCI, founder, Quad Graphics

In most workplaces, people still feel as if they're just a part of the means of production. Why? Because their leaders treat them that way.
> ←JIM STUART, cofounder, The Leadership Circle

Share your profits with all your associates, and treat them as partners. In turn, they will treat you as a partner, and together you will all perform beyond your widest expectations.
> ←SAM WALTON, founder, Wal-Mart

We have found what we believe to be the distilled essence of competitiveness. It is the reservoir of talent and creativity and energy that can be found in each of our people. That essence is liberated when we make people believe that what they think and do is important—and then get out of their way while they do it.
> ←JACK WELCH, chairman and CEO, General Electric

An overburdened, over-stretched executive is the best executive, because he or she doesn't have the time to meddle, to deal in trivia, to bother people.
> ←JACK WELCH

 *Marketing*

You can say the right thing about a product and nobody will listen. You've got to say it in such a way that people will feel it in their gut. Because if they don't feel it, nothing will happen.

—WILLIAM BERNBACH, cofounder, DDB Needham Advertising

Without push, pull's useless.

—MALCOLM FORBES, former publisher, *Forbes* magazine

Software suppliers are trying to make their software packages more "user friendly." … Their best approach, so far, has been to take all the old brochures and stamp the words "user friendly" on the cover.

—BILL GATES, founder and chairman, Microsoft

When the product is right, you don't have to be a great marketer.

—LEE IACOCCA, former chairman, Chrysler Corp.

The real trick to marketing is finding a core idea which the world can use. You find the universal, and then you make it the core of what you do.

—SHELLY LAZARUS, chairman and CEO, Ogilvy & Mather Advertising

Marketing is a very special view of the business process. It views the business enterprise as an organized process to create and keep a customer.

—THEODORE LEVITT, former editor, *Harvard Business Review,* and professor emeritus of business administration, Harvard University

We believe that our activities should be governed by the needs and desires of our customers rather than by our internal requirements and insights.

—EUGENE F. McCABE, VP marketing, Merke Sharpe & Dohme

I create markets.

    —Akio Morita, **former CEO, Sony Corp.**

Marketing is far too important to leave to the marketing department.

    —David Packard, **cofounder, Hewlett-Packard**

Strategy and timing are the Himalayas of marketing. Everything else is the Catskills.

    —Al Ries and Jack Trout, **consultants and coauthors,** *The Battle for your Mind*

No great marketing decisions have ever been made on quantitative data.

    —John Sculley, **former chairman, Apple Computer**

I am the world's worst salesman, therefore, I must make it easy for people to buy.

    —F. W. Woolworth, **founder, F. W. Woolworth Stores**

Tell them quick. Tell them often.

    —William Wrigley, Jr., **founder, William Wrigley Jr. Company**

Marketing is not about creating award-winning commercials.... For fast-food restaurants, it's about bites and slurps. For the airline, it's about butts in seats.

    —Sergio Zyman, **chief marketing officer, Coca-Cola**

Mistakes

To swear off making mistakes is very easy. All you have to do is swear off having ideas.

    —Leo Burnett, **founder, Leo Burnett Advertising**

When looking back, usually I'm more sorry for the things I didn't do than for the things I shouldn't have done.
— MALCOLM FORBES, former publisher, *Forbes* magazine

Freedom is not worth having if it does not connote freedom to err.
— MOHANDAS K. GANDHI, leader, Indian independence movement

A mistake is simply another way of doing things.
— KATHERINE GRAHAM, publisher, *The Washington Post*

The biggest mistake you can make in business is losing faith in people. Don't let a few who lie or backstab screw up your future.
— BUD HADFIELD, founder, Kwik Kopy, and chairman of the board, The International Center for Entrepreneurial Development

Our business world has accepted errors as a way of life. We live with them, we plan for them, and we make excuses for them. They have become part of the personality of our business. Our employees quickly recognize our standards and create errors so that they will not disappoint us.
— H. JAMES HARRINGTON, consultant and author

The best path to innovation is through what we call enlightened trial-and-error. The day starts, make a bunch of crummy prototypes and the next day show them to customers, users and manufacturing. They'll tell you what's wrong. Take copious notes and fix it.
— DAVID M. KELLEY, founder and CEO, IDEO

The trouble in America is not that we are making too many mistakes, but that we are making too few.
— PHIL KNIGHT, founder and chairman, Nike

We can afford almost any mistake once.

—LEWIS LEHR, president, 3M Company

While one person hesitates because he feels inferior, the other is busy making mistakes and becoming superior.

—HENRY C. LINK, author, *Employment Psychology* and *The Psychology of Selling and Advertising*, and coauthor, *The Fundamentals of Advertising*

Consider every mistake you do make as an asset.

—PAUL J. MEYER, founder, Success Motivation Institute, Inc. and Leadership Management International, Inc., author, *I Inherited a Fortune!*, and coauthor, *Bridging the Leadership Gap*

Don't be afraid to make a mistake. But make sure you don't make the same mistake twice.

—AKIO MORITA, former CEO, Sony Corp.

It is necessary for us to learn from others' mistakes. You will not live long enough to make them all yourself.

HYMAN G. RICKOVER, admiral and founder, the nuclear navy

Don't hide your failures and mistakes. Bury them in full public view with due humility and contrition. Who has the heart to castigate a repentant sinner?

—MILTON J. ROEDEL, manager, DuPont

A mistake is a value judgment rendered after the fact.

—JOHN WOODS, president, CWL Publishing Enterprises

The doctor can bury his mistakes but an architect can only advise his client to plant vines.

—FRANK LLOYD WRIGHT, architect

 *Money*

Money has a peculiar effect on people. If you're working hard for a salary that pays the rent and maybe lets you play around a little, then it's just money. But the first time you exercise your options and sell the shares you find out just how much money the government will take away from you, and you start to wonder what it is they're doing in Washington that's worth that much dough.

——STEWART ALSOP, Silicon Valley observer and writer

Money is a terrible master but an excellent servant.

——P. T. BARNUM, circus owner

I'm not a driven businessman, but a driven artist. I never think about money. Beautiful things make money.

——GEOFFREY BEENE, fashion designer and founder, Geoffrey Beene

Why shouldn't the American people take half my money from me? I took all of it from them.

——EDWARD A. FILENE, founder, Filene's Department Stores

The value of a pound is what the market says it is.

——MILTON FRIEDMAN, economist

If you can count your money, you don't have a billion dollars.

——J. PAUL GETTY, founder, Getty Oil

The maturing of any complex talent requires a happy combination of motivation, character and opportunity. Most talent remains undeveloped.

——JOHN GARDNER, founder, Common Cause

Money as money is nothing.

——H. L. HUNT, oil driller pioneer

The love of money as a possession—as distinguished from the love of money as a means to the enjoyments and realities of life—will be recognized for what it is, a somewhat disgusting morbidity, one of those semi-criminal, semi-pathological propensities, which one hands over with a shudder to the specialists in mental disease.

—JOHN MAYNARD KEYNES, economist

All money means to me is a pride in accomplishment.

—RAY KROC, chairman, McDonald's

Folks are serious about three things—their religion, their family, and most of all, their money.

—BERT LANCE, banker and director, Office of Management and Budget, Carter Administration

After a certain point money is meaningless. It ceases to be the goal. The game is what counts.

—ARISTOTLE ONASSIS, Greek ship owner and financier

Money never remains just coins and pieces of paper. Money can be translated into the beauty of living, a support in misfortune, an education, or future security. It also can be translated into a source of bitterness.

—SYLVIA PORTER, finance writer

Finance: the art of passing currency from hand to hand until it finally disappears.

—ROBERT W. SARNOFF, son of David Sarnoff and head of NBC

Money is a stupid measure of achievement, but unfortunately it is the only universal measure we have.

—CHARLES STEINMETZ, pioneering electrical engineer

No one would have remembered the Good Samaritan if he'd only had good intentions. He had money as well.

—MARGARET THATCHER, former Prime Minister, Great Britain

It's just as easy to be happy with a lot of money as with a little.
　—MARVIN TRAUB, CEO, Bloomingdale's

⇜ *Motivation* ⇝

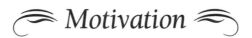

A desire to be observed, considered, esteemed, praised, beloved, and admired by his fellows is one of the earliest as well as the keenest dispositions discovered in the heart of man.
　—JOHN ADAMS, U.S. PRESIDENT

I'm slowly becoming a convert to the principle that you can't motivate people to do things, you can only demotivate them. The primary job of the manager is not to empower but to remove obstacles.
　—SCOTT ADAMS, Dilbert creator

Motivation will almost always beat mere talent.
　—NORMAN AUGUSTINE, CEO, Lockheed Martin

People who are unable to motivate themselves must be content with mediocrity, not matter how impressive their other talents.
　—ANDREW CARNEGIE, founder, U.S. Steel

People have inside of them a certain work ethic, and, if you appeal to them nicely, they'll respond and give all they can give.
　—FRED DELUCA, founder, Subway Sandwiches and Salads

Money motivates neither the best people, nor the best in people. It can move the body and influence the mind, but it cannot touch the heart or move the spirit; that is reserved for belief, principle, and morality.
　—DEE HOCK, founder and CEO emeritus, VISA USA and VISA International

It's not my job to motivate players. They bring extraordinary motivation to our program. It's my job not to de-motivate them.
—Lou Holtz, football coach, University of South Carolina

Ability is what you're capable of doing. Motivation determines what you do. Attitude determines how well you do it.
—Lou Holtz

All human beings prefer meaningful work to meaningless work.... If work is meaningless, life comes close to being meaningless.
—Abraham Maslow, psychologist and author, *Maslow on Management*

How do you motivate employees? You don't.
—Douglas McGregor, author and creator of "Theory X" and "Theory Y"

A man always has two reason for doing anything—a good reason and the real reason.
—J. Pierpont Morgan, American financier

You can get something done in a short time with fear, but in the long run it just doesn't pay off.
—Wendell Parsons, CEO, Stamp-Rite

Cutting [costs] isn't the answer—that can be done by stupid arbitrary judgments. Competitive companies must understand how to motivate people to be productive, and that is hard as hell.
—Andrew C. Sigler, chairman, Champion International Corporation

The Big Picture is all about motivation. It's giving people the reason for doing the job, the purpose of working. If you're going to play a game, you have to understand what it means to win. When you show people the Big Picture, you define winning.
—Jack Stack, CEO, Springfield Remanufacturing Corporation, and author, *The Great Game of Business*

Motivate your partners. Money and ownership aren't enough. Set high goals, encourage competition and then keep score. Make bets with outrageous payoffs.

— SAM WALTON, founder, Wal-Mart

We have to undo a 100-year-old concept and convince our managers that their role is not to control people and stay on top of things, but rather to guide, energize, and excite

— JACK WELCH, chairman and CEO, General Electric

You don't motivate people. You influence what they're motivated to do.

— JOHN WOODS, president, CWL Publishing Enterprises

People often say that motivation doesn't last. Well, neither does bathing—that's why we recommend it daily.

— ZIG ZIGLAR, founder, Ziglar Training Systems, and author

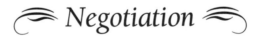 *Negotiation*

My father said: "You must never try to make all the money that's in a deal. Let the other fellow make some money too, because if you have a reputation for always making all the money, you won't have many deals."

— J. PAUL GETTY, founder, Getty Oil

A verbal contract isn't worth the paper it's printed on.

— SAMUEL GOLDWYN, cofounder, Metro-Goldwyn-Mayer Studios

You don't get what you deserve, you get what you negotiate.

— CHESTER KARRAS, author and negotiating skills trainer

Whenever you're sitting across from some important person, always picture him sitting there in a suit of long red underwear. That's the way I always operated in business.

——JOSEPH P. KENNEDY, **businessperson, ambassador, and father of John F. Kennedy**

Deals aren't usually blown by principals; they're blown by lawyers and accountants trying to prove how valuable they are.

——ROBERT TOWNSEND, **former CEO, Avis Rent-a-Car, and author,** *Up the Organization*

Networking

Networking is by far the most important aspect of business school. The classroom is a distant second.

——JAY DEVIVO, **head, UCLA Anderson School of Business Entrepreneurial Ventures Club**

Star performers know that effective networking means developing dependable two-way streets to the experts who help each other complete tasks critical to bottom-line results. Average performers think that networking is about hearing the latest office gossip or socializing for future job referrals.

——ROBERT KELLEY, **author,** *How to Be a Star at Work*

Networking is an enrichment program, not an entitlement program.

——SUSAN ROANE, **business consultant**

We found that we had a cool technology, good business ideas, and lots of ambition. But we also found that we lacked experience as well as industry visibility. We decided that networking was the best way to fill those gaps.

——SCOTT ROZIC, **CEO, Verge Software Corp**

By networking with several key headhunters, you become more of a three-dimensional person to them—instead of a hit-and-run job hunter.

➤ NANCY SCHRETTER, president, The Beacon Group

Opportunity

When one door closes another door opens; but we often look so long and so regretfully upon the closed door that we do not see the ones which open for us.

➤ ALEXANDER GRAHAM BELL, inventor of the telephone

The greater the rate of company expansion, the easier it is to find valuable new jobs for people.

➤ ED BERSOFF, founder, BTG, Inc.

Business opportunities are like buses, there's always another one coming.

➤ RICHARD BRANSON, founder, Virgin Group

You do things when the opportunities come along.

➤ WARREN BUFFET, CEO, Berkshire Hathaway

Many of the best jobs do not really exist until someone is hired for them.

➤ JAMES E. CHALLENGER, chief technology officer, Integrated Systems, Inc.

Results are gained by exploiting opportunities, not by solving problems.

➤ PETER F. DRUCKER, consultant and renowned management author

Opportunity is missed by most people because it is dressed in overalls and looks like work.

— THOMAS A. EDISON, American inventor

Look for opportunity. You can't wait for it to knock on the door.... You might not be home.

— JINGER HEATH, chairman, BeautiControl® Inc.

Procrastination is opportunity's natural assassin.

— VICTOR KIAM, CEO, Remington Products

There is no security on this earth; there is only opportunity.

— DOUGLAS MACARTHUR, general, World War II

I feel that the greatest reward for doing is the opportunity to do more.

— DR. JONAS SALK, developer of the salk polio vaccine and founder, the Salk Institute

If a window of opportunity appears, don't pull down the shade.

— TOM PETERS, author and consultant

Perhaps the most important thing that has come out of my life is the discovery that if you prepare yourself at every point as well as you can, with whatever means you have, however meager they may seem, you will be able to grasp opportunity for broader experience when it appears. Without preparation you cannot do it.

— ELEANOR ROOSEVELT, former First Lady

All the American women had purple noses and gray lips and their faces were chalk white from terrible powder. I recognized that the United States could be my life's work.

— HELENA RUBINSTEIN, founder and president, Helena Rubinstein, Inc.

Each problem has hidden in it an opportunity so powerful that it literally dwarfs the problem. The greatest success stories were created by people who recognized a problem and turned it into an opportunity.

━JOSEPH SUGARMAN, chairman, JS&A, Inc.

The more you seek security, the less of it you have. But the more you seek opportunity, the more likely it is that you will achieve the security that you desire.

━BRIAN TRACY, speaker, consultant and trainer

Perseverance

One of the things I learned the hard way was it does not pay to get discouraged. Keeping busy and making optimism a way of life can restore your faith in yourself.

━LUCILLE BALL, actress and head of DesiLu Studios

Try as we may, none of us can be free of conflict and woe. Even the greatest men have had to accept disappointments as their daily bread…. The art of living lies less in eliminating our troubles than in growing with them.

━BERNARD BARUCH, American financier and presidential advisor

Most of the important things in the world have been accomplished by people who have kept on trying when there seemed to be no hope at all.

━DALE CARNEGIE, author, *How to Win Friends and Influence People*

The key to building an enduring new medium is passion, people, perseverance, perspective and paranoia."

━STEVE CASE, founder and chairman, America Online

Never give up. Never give up. Never, never, never.
  —WINSTON CHURCHILL, **former Prime Minister, Great Britain**

I'm hard-nosed about luck. I think it sucks. ... If you're persistent in trying and doing and working, you almost make your own fortune.
  —JERRY DELLA FEMINA, **founder, Della Femina Travisano & Partners and Jerry, Inc.**

No one would have crossed the ocean if he could have gotten off the ship in the storm.
  —CHARLES F. KETTERING, **president, General Motors Research Corp., and cofounder, Sloan-Kettering Institute for Cancer Research**

Press on. Nothing in the world can take the place of persistence.
  —RAY KROC, **founder, McDonald's**

Once you learn to quit, it becomes a habit.
  —VINCE LOMBARDI, **legendary coach, Green Bay Packers**

A man is not finished when he's defeated; he's finished when he quits.
  —RICHARD M. NIXON, **U.S. President**

Something in human nature causes us to start slacking off at our moment of greatest accomplishment. As you become successful, you will need a great deal of self-discipline not to lose your sense of balance, humility, and commitment.
  —H. ROSS PEROT, **founder, EDS and Perot Systems**

If you keep working at it, in the last analysis, you win.... They've got to kill us a hundred times. All we have to do is kill them once.
  —FREDERICK SMITH, **founder and chairman, Federal Express**

I had to pick myself up and get on with it, do it all over again, only even better this time.
  —SAM WALTON, **founder, Wal-Mart**

No mistake or failure is as bad as to stop and not try again.

━JOHN WANAMAKER, founder, Wanamaker Department Stores

Always continue the climb. It is possible for you to do whatever you choose, if you first get to know who you are and are willing to work with a power that is greater than ourselves to do it.

━OPRAH WINFREY, businesswoman and television talk show host

Personnel Development

Mentors … guide their disciples … imparting the wisdom they have acquired over many years…. Godfathers—sometimes called "rabbis"—are in a position to intervene on your behalf; by definition, they are powerful people with an interest in your career.

━MARY ANN ALLISON, principal, The Allison Group, LLC

If our people develop faster than a competitor's people, then they're worth more.

━JAMES M. BIGGAR, chairman & CEO, Nestlé Enterprises, Inc.

To be a manager, you have to start at the bottom—no exceptions.

━HENRY BLOCK, founder, H&R Block, Inc.

I think you've got to continuously make sure [employees] understand how important they are. As a CEO, you need people more than they need you. My job is to keep our people interested in staying, and working, and growing and prospering with this company.

━LAWRENCE BOSSIDY, chairman, Honeywell

It is only as we develop others that we permanently succeed.
—HARVEY S. FIRESTONE, founder, Firestone Rubber

It's the CEO's job to trigger thinking by creating events or questions to get people's wheels spinning.
—MARCEL LeBRUN, president and CEO, iMagicTV

The ultimate leader is one who is willing to develop people to the point that they surpass him or her in knowledge and ability.
— FRED A. MANSKE, JR., author, *Secrets of Effective Leadership*

Get the best people and train them well.
—CHARLES MERRILL, founder, Merrill Lynch & Co.

We decided the best way to become the customer's restaurant of choice was to become the employer of choice. Our plan on this front was two-pronged: to work harder to develop the potential of the people we already had, and to move aggressively to attract and retain the best people we could find.
—JAMES NEAR, chairman and CEO, Wendy's International

I never had a boss that tried to sit on me, and I think that's essential. If you expect people to develop, you have to give them the responsibility, you have to tell them what their objectives are and you have to let them do it.
—DAVID M. RODMAN, partner, Arthur Andersen Consulting

If we let our people flourish and grow, unleash people to be self-confident and take on more responsibility, if we use the best ideas they come up with, then we will have a chance to win. The idea of liberation and empowerment for our work force is not enlightenment; it's a competitive necessity.
—JACK WELCH, chairman and CEO, General Electric

 *Planning*

We can't cross a bridge until we come to it; but I always like to lay down a pontoon ahead of time.
— BERNARD BARUCH, American financier and presidential advisor

It's not the will to win, but the will to prepare to win that makes the difference.
— PAUL "BEAR" BRYANT, former football coach, University of Alabama

Plan the sale when you plan the ad.
— LEO BURNETT, founder, Leo Burnett Advertising

Make no little plans. They have no magic to stir men's blood and probably themselves will not be realized.
— DANIEL H. BURNHAM, architect, partner, Burnham & Root, and founder, D.H. Burnham & Company

I learned that, before you reach an objective, you must be ready with a new one, and you must start to communicate it to the organization. But it is not the goal itself that is important.
— JAN CARLZON, former CEO, SAS, and author, *The Moment of Truth*

Long range planning does not deal with future decisions but with the future of present decisions.
— PETER F. DRUCKER, consultant and renowned management author

In preparing for battle I have always found that plans are useless, but planning is indispensable.
— DWIGHT D. EISENHOWER, U.S. President

I knew I loved making cookies and every time I did, I made people happy. That was my business plan.
— DEBBI FIELDS, founder, Mrs. Fields' Cookies

Nobody can really guarantee the future. The best we can do is size up the chances, calculate the risks involved, estimate our ability to deal with them and then make our plans with confidence.

— HENRY FORD, II, **former chairman, Ford Motor Company**

Planning for happiness is rarely successful. Happiness just happens.

— ROBERT HALF, **founder, Robert Half International**

I object to people running down the future. I am going to live the rest of my life there, and I'd like it to be a nice place.

— CHARLES F. KETTERING, **president, General Motors Research Corp., and cofounder, Sloan-Kettering Institute for Cancer Research**

People don't plan to fail. They fail to plan.

— MARK MCCORMACK, **founder and CEO, International Management Group**

The only thing that matters is cash flow—not the cash flows they use today, but the old cash flows that laid out the source and application of funds—where it's coming from and where it's going and how much is left over. No company has ever gone bankrupt because it had a loss on its P&L.

— WILLIAM G. MCGOWAN, **founder, MCI Communications**

Success or failure is often determined on the drawing board.

— ROBERT J. MCKAIN, **author,** *Realize Your Potential*

A good plan provides direction for action, but, sometimes even more, it provides a baseline to help you understand what actually happens.

— JOHN WOODS, **president, CWL Publishing Enterprises**

Power

Do you know what amazes me more than anything else? The impotence of force to organize anything. There are only two powers in the world—the spirit and the sword—and in the long run the sword will always be conquered by the spirit.

—NAPOLEON BONAPARTE, former emperor of France

Power is the faculty or capacity to act, the strength and potency to accomplish something. It is the vital energy to make choices and decision. It also includes the capacity to overcome deeply embedded habits and to cultivate higher, more effective ones.

—STEPHEN R. COVEY, consultant and author, *The 7 Habits of Highly Effective People*

The more you are talked about the less powerful you are.

—BENJAMIN DISRAELI, 19th century Prime Minister, Great Britain

Those carried away by power are soon carried away.

—MALCOLM FORBES, former publisher, *Forbes* magazine

I have never been able to conceive how any rational being could propose happiness to himself from the exercise of power over others.

—THOMAS JEFFERSON, U.S. President

When power leads man to arrogance, poetry reminds him of his limitation. When power narrows the area of man's concern, poetry reminds him of the richness and diversity of his existence. When power corrupts, poetry cleanses.

—JOHN F. KENNEDY, U.S. President

Far too many executives have become more concerned with the "four P's"—pay, perks, power and prestige—rather than making profits for shareholders.

—T. BOONE PICKENS, founder, Mesa Petroleum Co.

No one has power except as it is accorded them by others, and they only do that when it's in their best interest. If you want to maintain your power, make sure you look out for the interests of those who gave it to you, both those above you and those below.

—JOHN WOODS, president, CWL Publishing Enterprises

≈ *Problem Solving* ≈

We teach collaborative problem-solving. In school that's called cheating.

—EDWARD BALES, director of education, Motorola home office

If your project doesn't work, look for the part that you didn't think was important.

—ARTHUR BLOCH, author, books about Murphy's Law

Problems are solved on the spot, as soon as they arise. No front-line employee has to wait for a supervisor's permission.

—JAN CARLZON, former president, Scandinavian Airlines, and author, *Moments of Truth*

The measure of success is not whether you have a tough problem to deal with, but whether it's the same problem you had last year.

—JOHN FOSTER DULLES, Secretary of State, Eisenhower Administration

Problems always appear bigger when incompetent men are working on them.

—WILLIAM FEATHER, editor and publisher, *The William Feather Magazine*, and author, *As We Were Saying*

Life is a continuous exercise in creative problem solving.

—MICHAEL J. GELB, speaker and trainer on creativity and leadership

Asking the right questions takes as much skill as giving the right answers.
  —ROBERT HALF, founder, Robert Half International

The post-heroic manager asks how every problem can be solved in a way that develops other people's capacity to handle it.
  —CHARLES HANDY, cofounder, London Business School, and author, *Understanding Organizations* and *Beyond Certainty: The Changing Worlds of Organizations*

The only thing that matters is the bottom line? What a presumptuous thing to say. The bottom line's in heaven. The real business of business is building things.
  —EDWIN LAND, founder, Polaroid Corp.

When the only tool you have is a hammer you tend to see every problem as a nail.
  —ABRAHAM MASLOW, psychologist and author, *Maslow on Management*

The best way to view a present problem is to give *it* all you've got, to study it and its nature, to perceive *within* it the intrinsic interrelationships, to discover (rather than to invent) the answer to the problem within the problem itself.
  —ABRAHAM MASLOW

Most communications problems can be solved with proximity.
  —RICHARD A. MORAN, author, *Never Confuse a Memo With Reality: And Other Business Lessons Too Simple Not to Know* and *Fear No Yellow Stickies: More Business Wisdom Too Simple Not to Know*

We have always found that people are most productive in small teams with tight budgets, time lines, and the freedom to solve their own problems.
  —JOHN ROLLWAGEN, former chairman and CEO, Cray Computer

The best way out of a problem is through it.
  —UNKNOWN

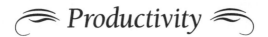

Productivity

The productivity of work is not the responsibility of the worker but of the manager.
—PETER DRUCKER, **consultant and renowned management author**

Stressing output is the key to improving productivity, while looking to increase activity can result in just the opposite.
—ANDREW S. GROVE, **former CEO, Intel Corp.**

Productivity is being able to do things that you were never able to do before.
—JIM MANZI, **president, Lotus Development**

Nothing makes a person more productive than the last minute.
—UNKNOWN

We know where most of the creativity, the innovation, the stuff that drives productivity lies—in the minds of those closest to the work. It's been there in front of our noses all along while we've been running around chasing robots and reading books on how to become Japanese—or at least manage like them
—JACK WELCH, **chairman and CEO, General Electric**

Profit

It isn't high prices that persuade the high cost and marginal producer to make the investment necessary to bring him into production. It is the promise of profit. High prices without profit merely requires more investment to support turnover and inventory.
—BERNARD BARUCH, **American financier and presidential advisor**

And I have one last rule: Obey Friedman's law and make a profit. That will create jobs, and that is the most revolutionary concept there is.

—THORNTON F. BRADSHAW, **president, Atlantic Richfield Company**

I don't want to do business with those who don't make a profit, because they can't give the best service.

—LEE BRISTOL, **founder, Bristol-Meyers**

Profits are to a corporation what breathing is to human life. We cannot live in a private enterprise system without profits. But breathing is not the sole purpose of life, and profits are not the sole purpose of the adventure that we call business management.

—FLETCHER BYROM, **former president, Koppers Co.**

It is a socialist idea that making profits is a vice; I consider the real vice is making losses.

—WINSTON CHURCHILL, **former Prime Minister, Great Britain**

Profitability is a necessary condition for existence and a means to more important ends, but it is not the end in itself for many of the visionary companies. Profit is like oxygen, food, water, and blood for the body; they are not the *point* of life, but without them, there is no life.

—JAMES C. COLLINS AND JERRY I. PORRAS, **authors,** *Built to Last*

The profit motive and its offspring maximization of profits are ... irrelevant to the function of a business, the purpose of a business, and the job of managing a business.

—PETER F. DRUCKER, **consultant and renowned management author**

If an exchange between two parties is voluntary, it will not take place unless both believe they will benefit from it. Most economic fallacies derive from the neglect of this simple insight, from the tendency to assume that there is a fixed pie, that one party can gain only at the expense of another.

—MILTON FRIEDMAN, **economist**

In a recent study, more than 80 percent of executives said they believed managers choose profits over what's right, when forced to decide between the two.

→SETH GODIN, **founder and president, Yoyodyne Entertainment, and vice president, Direct Marketing, Yahoo!**

The worst crime against working people is a company which fails to operate at a profit.

→SAMUEL GOMPERS, **early labor leader**

The only way to keep score in business is to add up how much money you make.

→HARRY B. HELMSLEY, **real estate developer**

When someone asked me, which do you put first in your mind, service or profits, I said naturally I put service first, but we can only serve by earning money.

→FREDERICK R. KAPPEL, **former president, AT&T**

To call profit the goal of the corporation is operationally silly. It is like saying that the goal of human life is eating. Profit, like eating, is a requisite, not a purpose.

→THEODORE LEVITT, **former editor,** *Harvard Business Review,* **and professor emeritus of business administration, Harvard University**

A business should quickly stand on its own based on the service it provides society. Profits should be a reflection not of corporate greed but a vote of confidence from society that what is offered by the firm is valued.

→KONOSUKE MATSUSHITA, **founder, Matsushita Electric Co.**

Putting profits after people and products was magical at Ford.

→DON PETERSEN, **former CEO, Ford Motor Company**

The short-term and frequently shortsighted positions win out with disturbing regularity because American business is top-heavy with the ever-expanding numbers of business school graduates who are trained advocates of the short-term profit.

　—MICHAEL P. SCHULHOF, former president, Sony USA

If we had to point out one single notion which is calculated to damage our industrial performance, to prevent us from competing effectively in the world and ultimately to undermine the basis of a free and diverse society, it is the idea that profit is somehow wrong.

　—MARGARET THATCHER, former Prime Minister, Great Britain

Profits are the organization's measure of the benefits and quality it has delivered to customers. So are losses.

　—JOHN WOODS, president, CWL Publishing Enterprises

Profits are not what's left over after all the other expenses are paid. Profits also represent a cost: the cost of keeping the organization whole.

　—JOHN WOODS

Progress

The *Fortune* 500 is over.

　—PETER F. DRUCKER, consultant and renowned management author

Restlessness and discontent are the first necessities of progress.

　—THOMAS A. EDISON, American inventor

Yesterday's miracle is today's intolerable condition.

　—LEWIS D. EIGEN, executive VP, University Research Corporation

One fact stands out in bold relief in the history of man's attempts for betterment. That is that when compulsion is used, only resentment is aroused, and the end is not gained. Only through moral suasion and appeal to man's reason can a movement succeed.

—SAMUEL GOMPERS, early labor leader

The slogan of progress is changing from the full dinner pail to the full garage.

—HERBERT HOOVER, U.S. President

The price of progress is trouble.

—CHARLES F. KETTERING, president, General Motors Research Corp., and cofounder, Sloan-Kettering Institute for Cancer Research

The means by which we live have outdistanced the ends for which we live. Our scientific power has outrun our spiritual power. We have guided missiles and misguided me.

—MARTIN LUTHER KING, JR., American civil rights leader

If necessity is the mother of invention, discontent is the father of progress.

—DAVID ROCKERFELLER, former chairman, Chase Manhattan Bank

If we hadn't put a man on the moon, there wouldn't be a Silicon Valley today.

—JOHN SCULLEY, former chairman, Apple Computer

Some have an idea that the reason we in this country discard things so readily is because we have so much. The facts are exactly opposite—the reason we have so much is simply because we discard things so readily. We replace the old in return for something that will serve us better.

—ALFRED P. SLOAN, JR., president and CEO, General Motors, 1923-1946

Whenever an individual or a business decides that success has been attained, progress stops.

— THOMAS J. WATSON, SR., founder, IBM

The winners of the nineties will be those who can develop a culture that allows them to move faster, communicate more clearly, and involve everyone in a focused effort to serve ever more demanding customers.

— JACK WELCH, chairman and CEO, General Electric

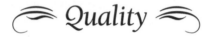

Quality

Anybody can cut prices, but it takes brains to produce a better article.

— PHILIP D. ARMOUR, founder, Armour & Co.

The [quality control] issue has more to do with people and motivation and less to do with capital and equipment than one would think.

— MICHAEL BEER, author and professor, Harvard Business School

The surest foundation of a manufacturing concern is quality. After that, and a long way after that, comes cost.

— ANDREW CARNEGIE, founder, U.S. Steel

Quality is determined by top management. It cannot be delegated.

— W. EDWARDS DEMING, consultant and author, *Out of the Crisis*

Efficiency is doing better what is already being done.

— PETER F. DRUCKER, consultant and renowned management author

Quality is not only right, it is free. And it is not only free, it is the most profitable product line we have.

— HAROLD GENEEN, former CEO, IT&T

Quality isn't asserted by the supplier; it's perceived by the customer.

> ━JOHN GUASPARI, consultant and author, *I Know It When I See It*

Give them quality. That's the best kind of advertising.

> ━MILTON HERSHEY, founder, Hershey Chocolate Co.

Styling and value are what sells cars, but quality is what keeps them sold.

> ━LEE IACOCCA, former chairman, Chrysler Corp.

Quality control is applicable to any kind of enterprise. In fact, it must be applied in every enterprise.

> ━KAORU ISHIKAWA, professor, Tokyo University, founder, Union of Japanese Scientists and Engineers, president, Musashi Institute of Technology, and author, *Guide to Quality Control* and *What Is Total Quality Control?*

Be a yardstick of quality. Some people aren't used to an environment where excellence is expected.

> ━STEVEN JOBS, founder and CEO, Apple Computer

Quality does not happen by accident; it has to be planned.

> ━JOSEPH M. JURAN, consultant and founder, The Juran Institute

The product that will not sell without advertising will not sell profitably with advertising.

> ━ALBERT LASKER, early 20th century advertising executive

Imperfect products should be available because consumers have different preferences for defect avoidance.

> ━JAMES MILLER, consultant and speaker

Almost all quality improvement comes via simplification of design, manufacturing, layout, processes, and procedures.

> ━TOM PETERS, author and consultant

I think quality control is an oxymoron. True quality needs space to breathe. If quality is built in, then where's the need for control? Why on earth would you want to control quality? It should be allowed to run rampant.

—HAL F. ROSENBLUTH, chairman and CEO, Rosenbluth Travel

Quality is not any single thing but an aura, an atmosphere, an over-powering feeling that a company is doing everything with excellence.

—JACK WELCH, chairman and CEO, General Electric

 *Responsibility*

It means the substitution of responsibility for obedience to rank, and of authority of performance for the authority of rank.

—PETER DRUCKER, consultant and renowned management author

An executive cannot gradually dismiss details. Business is made up of details, and I notice that the chief executive who dismisses them is quite likely to dismiss his business.

—HARVEY S. FIRESTONE, founder, Firestone Rubber Co.

If we had failed to pursue the facts as far as they led, we would have denied the public any knowledge of an unprecedented scheme of political surveillance and sabotage.

—KATHERINE GRAHAM, publisher, *The Washington Post*

The search for someone to blame is always successful.

—ROBERT HALF, founder, Robert Half International

We must exchange the philosophy of excuse—what I am is beyond my control—for the philosophy of responsibility.
> —BARBARA JORDAN, **lawyer and former member of congress**

Success on any major scale requires you to accept responsibility.... In the final analysis, the one quality that all successful people have ... is the ability to take on responsibility.
> —MICHAEL KORDA, **author,** *Success* **and** *Power! How to Use It, How to Get It*

The disappearance of a sense of responsibility is the most far-reaching consequence of submission to authority.
> —STANLEY MILGRAM, **author,** *Obedience to Authority*

The buck stops with the guy who signs the checks.
> —RUPERT MURDOCH, **founder and chairman, The News Corp.**

It is important to admit your mistakes, and to do so before you are charged with them. Many clients are surrounded by buckpassers who make a fine art of blaming the agency for their own failures. I seize the earliest opportunity to assume the blame.
> —DAVID OGILVY, **cofounder, Ogilvy & Mather Advertising**

I believe that every right implies a responsibility; every opportunity, an obligation; every possession, a duty.
> —JOHN D. ROCKEFELLER, JR., **U.S. oil magnate and philanthropist**

In your area of responsibility, if you do not control events, you are at the mercy of events.
> —HARLAN SVARE, **former head coach, San Diego Chargers**

If you let decisions be made for you, you'll be trampled.
> —BETSY WHITE, **manager, Ocean Spray**

Risk

Most people live and die with their music still unplayed. They never dare to try.

—MARY KAY ASH, founder, Mary Kay Cosmetics

I don't want to give the impression that our future success is assured. I believe the opposite. I believe our future success is *not* assured. If you look at the history of the pioneers, it's not good.

—JEFF BEZOS, founder, Amazon.com

Risk comes from not knowing what you're doing.

—WARREN BUFFET, CEO, Berkshire Hathaway

We don't grow unless we take risks. Any successful company is riddled with failures.

—JAMES E. BURKE, former chairman of the board and CEO, Johnson & Johnson

There's as much risk in doing nothing as in doing something.

—TRAMMELL CROW, founder, Trammell Crow Company

You can't run a business without taking risks.

—MILLARD DREXLER, president and CEO, Gap Inc.

Venture nothing, and life is less than it should be.

—MALCOLM FORBES, former publisher, *Forbes* magazine

Don't be afraid to take a big step when one is indicated. You can't cross a chasm in two small jumps.

—DAVID LLOYD GEORGE, Prime Minister, Great Britain, 1916-1922

When you bet on a sure thing—hedge!

—ROBERT HALF, founder, Robert Half International

Every business and every product has risks. You can't get around it.
— LEE IACOCCA, **former chairman, Chrysler Corp.**

It's better to be boldly decisive and risk being wrong than to agonize at length and be right too late.
— MARILYN MOATS KENNEDY, **managing partner, Career Strategies**

The policy of being too cautious is the greatest risk of all.
— JAWAHARLAL NEHRU, **first Prime Minister, India**

Educated risks are the key to success.
— WILLIAM OLSTEN, **CEO, Olsten Services Corporation**

Take calculated risks. That is quite different from being rash.
— GEORGE S. PATTON, **World War II general**

If you're not a risk taker, you should get the hell out of business.
— STEVEN J. ROSS, **former chairman, Time Warner**

Growth means change and change involves risk, stepping from the known to the unknown.
— GEORGE SHINN, **chairman of the board, Shinn Enterprises, Inc., and owner, Charlotte Hornets**

A gambler is some one who plays slot machines. I prefer to own slot machines.
— DONALD TRUMP, **chairman, The Trump Organization**

Every time we've moved ahead in IBM, it was because someone was willing to take a chance, put his head on the block, and try something new.
— THOMAS J. WATSON, JR., **son of founder and former chairman, IBM**

 Sales and Selling

Sell practical, tested merchandise at reasonable profit, treat your customers like human beings—and they will always come back.

➤ L.L. BEAN, founder, L.L. Bean Company

Sell cheap and tell the truth.

➤ ROSE BLUMKIN, founder, Nebraska Furniture Mart

There is no such thing as soft sell and hard sell. There is only smart sell and stupid sell.

➤ CHARLES BROWDER, former president of Batten, Barton, Durstine, and Osborn (BBDO)

Anyone who thinks that people can be fooled or pushed around has an inaccurate and pretty low estimate of people—and he won't do very well in advertising.

➤ LEO BURNETT, founder, Leo Burnett Advertising

It is not the purpose of the ad or commercial to make the reader or listener say, "My, what a clever ad." It is the purpose of advertising to make the reader or listener say, "I believe I'll buy one when I'm shopping tomorrow."

➤ MORRIS HITE, chair 1950-1982, Tracy-Locke advertising agency (now DDB Needham)

Evangelism is selling a dream.

➤ GUY KAWASAKI, former evangelist, Apple, CEO, garage.com, and author, *Rules for Revolutionaries*, *Selling the Dream*, and *How to Drive Your Competition Crazy*

If you don't sell, it's not the product that's wrong, it's you.

➤ ESTÉE LAUDER, founder, CEO, and chairman of the board, Estée Lauder

If eighty percent of your sales come from twenty percent of all of your items, just carry those twenty percent.

　　—STEW LEONARD, founder and president, Stew Leonard's Inc.

In selling as in medicine, prescription before diagnosis is malpractice.

　　—JOHN NAISBITT, former executive with IBM and Eastman Kodak, and author, *Megatrends*, *Global Paradox*, and *High Tech/High Touch*

We are all salesmen every day of our lives. We are selling our ideas, our plans, our enthusiasms to those with whom we come in contact.

　　—CHARLES M. SCHWAB, former CEO, Bethlehem Steel

Selling art has a lot to do with selling root beer.

　　—A. ALFRED TAUBMAN, chairman, CEO, and director, The Taubman Company, and chairman and director, Sotheby's

Salesmanship is an American specialty. It typifies the competitive spirit of our economy. Nowhere else in the world have so many executives come up through the selling ranks.

　　—ROBERT WHITNEY, president, New York Stock Exchange

You never sell anything to anyone. You just facilitate them selling it to themselves.

　　—JOHN WOODS, president, CWL Publishing Enterprises

Every sale has five basic obstacles: no need, no money, no hurry, no desire, no trust.

　　—ZIG ZIGLAR, founder, Ziglar Training Systems, and author

Startups

It's strange trying to scale a culture with such ferocious speed. What startups do these days—growing from nothing to hundreds of people overnight—simply isn't natural. There's nothing evolutionary about it. In fact, it's painful. But if you can pull it off, it's an amazing feeling.

—ANDREW BEEBE, cofounder, chairman, and CEO of Bigstep.com

There have been some dramatic hiccups in my life. If you start a company from scratch, and you don't have any financial backing, the only thing that matters is survival. And you have close shaves.

—RICHARD BRANSON, founder, Virgin Group

Before you even get started, there has to be absolute enthusiasm about the idea behind the business. And love of the subject matter has to exist organizationwide: Those who will provide the capital have to share your vision.

—LOU DOBBS, founder, chairman, and CEO, Space.com

My philosophy is simple: Love what you do. Don't do something because you hear that it's a great way to make money.

—RICHARD FOOS, president, Rhino Records

The dirty little secret of startups is that people get popped out of them all the time—even the founders. This is not something that they tell you when you start your own company: Your company may survive, but you may not.

—MARY FURLONG, founder, ThirdAge Media

The secret to success is to start from scratch and keep on scratching.

—DENNIS GREEN, coach, Minnesota Vikings

Start with good people, lay out the rules, communicate with your employees, motivate them and reward them. If you do all those things effectively, you can't miss.

—Lee Iacocca, former chairman, Chrysler Corp.

When you're starting a business from scratch, speed is everything. Keeping the board small and concentrated really helps. You don't have to manage the interrelationships between board members.

—Timothy A. Koogle, founder and chief executive, Yahoo!

The key to a successful startup is networking—both personal and professional. Money is just money. Who invests is more important than how much is invested.

—Regis McKenna, chairman, The McKenna Group

In a start-up company, you basically throw out all assumptions every three weeks.

—Scott McNealy, CEO, Sun Microsystems, Inc.

You look at any giant corporation, and I mean the biggies, and they all started with a guy with an idea, doing it well.

—Irvine Robbins, cofounder, Baskin-Robbins Ice Cream

Don't squander great ideas and great people on trying to enter a shrinking market. Play in a big market, no matter how difficult the competition may be.

—Rick Shriner, CEO, Exponential Technology

Startups don't have the luxury of time. You have to put your personal life on hold, and you have to dedicate yourself 200% to making your dream a reality.

—Ivonne Valdes, VP sales, Exponential Technology

Here are three rules for startups. First, have a differentiated product or service. Second, obtain capital of the highest quality, so that your money will open doors for you. Third, show that your company is able to evolve.

→ ANDREA WILLIAMS, **managing director, Equity Research E*Offering Corp.**

Success

The successful man is the one who had the chance and took it.

→ ROGER BABSON, **founder, Babson-United, Inc.**

The great pleasure in life is doing what people say you cannot do.

→ WALTER BAGEHOT, **founding editor,** *The Economist*

In a nutshell, the key to success is identifying those unique modules of talent within you and then finding the right arena to use them.

→ WARREN BENNIS, **founder and chair, Leadership Institute, University of Southern California**

The more you enjoy your job, and the more you want to outwork everyone else, the more likely you'll make an invaluable contribution to your organization—and succeed.

→ MICHAEL BLOOMBERG, **founder and chairman, Bloomberg L.P.**

Success is when something you've said or something you've written enters the public discourse—usually without your name attached. It becomes something people find worth saying to one another on its own merits.

→ STEWART BRAND, **cofounder, Global Business Network**

Success means never letting the competition define you. Instead, you have to define yourself based on a point of view you care deeply about.

— TOM CHAPPEL, cofounder and president, Tom's of Maine

Success seems to be largely a matter of hanging on after others have let go.

— WILLIAM FEATHER, editor and publisher, *The William Feather Magazine*, and author, *As We Were Saying*

Success Factors for Microsoft:
1. Long term approach
2. Passion for products and technology
3. Teamwork
4. Results
5. Customer feedback
6. Individual excellence

1&4, 2&5, 3&6 should work to balance each other.

— BILL GATES, founder and chairman, Microsoft

Once you think you can write down what made you successful, you won't be.

— LOU GERSTNER, chairman and CEO, IBM

My formula for success? Rise early, work late, strike oil.

— J. PAUL GETTY, founder, Getty Oil

An organization's success has enormously more to do with clarity of a shared purpose, common principles and strength of belief in them than to assets, expertise, operating ability, or management competence, important as they may be.

— DEE HOCK, founder and CEO emeritus, VISA USA and VISA International

True artists ship.

— STEVE JOBS, cofounder and chairman, Apple Computer

I know that in the final analysis, workaholics are not business successes.

— Patti Manuel, president and COO, long-distance division, Sprint

The success or failure of a company is determined as much by the fortunes of the marketplace as by the management. You can have an extremely good CEO of a failing company.

— Archie Norman, chair, ASDA Group plc (UK) supermarket chain, and Member of Parliament

To be successful, keep looking tanned, live in an elegant building (even if you're in the cellar), be seen in smart restaurants (even if you nurse one drink) and if you borrow, borrow big.

— Aristotle Onassis, Greek shipowner and financier

Life is pretty simple: You do some stuff. Most fails. Some works. You do more of what works. If it works big, others quickly copy it. Then you do something else. The trick is the doing something else.

— Tom Peters, author and consultant

I don't measure my "success" every day. I measure how much we have left to do. In that sense, business success is just a form of persistence.

— Daniel Snyder, president and CEO, Snyder Communications Inc.

Success should be measured by objective standards of competitive achievement. That means for runners: How fast are you? For business people: How much profit did you earn? For politicians: How many votes did you get? That is success.

— Bonnie St. John Deane, author, *Succeeding Sane*

The most important ingredient for success is the willingness to fail, to be made a fool of, to fall on your face a hundred times a day. And to be dumb. What makes repeated failure endurable is being in love with the work you do and being convinced of its value. Then the process becomes self-rewarding.

— Helen Tworkov, founding editor, *Tricycle: The Buddhist Review*

 *Teams*

The important thing to recognize is that it takes a team, and a team ought to get the credit. Successes have many fathers—failures none.
—PHILIP CALDWELL, **former chairman, Ford Motor Company**

The best way to build, support and retain a great team is to encourage a rockin' culture that everyone wants to be part of!
—CHRISTINE COMAFORD, **founder, planet U and Artemis Ventures**

Coming together is a beginning. Keeping together is progress. Working together is success.
—HENRY FORD, **founder, Ford Motor Company**

If you really believe in quality, when you cut through everything, it's empowering your people, and it's empowering your people that leads to teams.
—JAMIE HOUGHTON, **former chairman, Corning, Inc.**

For people to treat each other as teammates, they have to believe it is in their best interests to cooperate; they must be more concerned with how the system as a whole operates than with optimizing their own little piece.
—BRIAN JOINER, **author,** *Fourth Generation Management*

Superior work teams recognize that consistently high performance can be built not on rules but only on values.
—DENNIS KINLAW, **author,** *Coaching for Commitment*

There's a sort of unconditional love that develops when you're a mother. You believe in people, and you accept their weaknesses, their frailties, their moments of irrationality. That's what helps build very strong teams.
—SHELLY LAZARUS, **chairman and CEO, Ogilvy & Mather Advertising**

Individual commitment to a group effort—that is what makes a team work, a company work, a society work, a civilization work.
—VINCE LOMBARDI, **legendary coach, Green Bay Packers**

A well-run restaurant is like a winning baseball team. It makes the most of every crew member's talent and takes advantage of every split-second opportunity to speed up service.
—DAVID OGILVY, **cofounder, Ogilvy & Mather Advertising**

Great people don't equal great teams.
—TOM PETERS, **author and consultant**

Teams are less likely [than individuals] to overlook key issues and problems or take the wrong actions.
—EUGENE RAUDSEPP, **author,** *Managing Creative Scientists and Engineers*

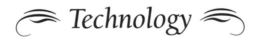

Technology

In the next wave, *Fortune* 500 companies will make 'e' such a core part of their business that the difference between 'e' and everything else will be nonexistent. Or they won't be in business anymore.
—STEWART ALSOP, **Silicon Valley observer and writer**

One of the only ways to compete is with technology.
—JOHN H. BEAKES, **cofounder, president, and chief operating officer, RWD Technologies**

Silicon Valley speed is different from *Fortune* 500 speed.
—DENIS BEAUSEJOUR, **VP, Procter & Gamble**

The factory of the future will have only two employees, a man and a dog. The man will be there to feed the dog. The dog will be there to keep the man from touching the equipment.

—WARREN BENNIS, founder and chair, Leadership Institute, University of Southern California

In many instances, a properly motivated person can outperform a robot. That high level of performance, however, could never, and likely should never, be sustained by a person day in and day out.

—TERRY FEULNER, section head, Hughes Aircraft Company

History teaches us… that by and large workers displaced by technological advance have moved rapidly into other employment, ultimately to better-paying jobs. This is why we have had rising personal incomes rather than mass unemployment as new technology has come into use and productivity has increased.

—HENRY FORD, II, former chairman and grandson of founder, Ford Motor Company

The first rule of any technology used in a business is that automation applied to an efficient operation will magnify the efficiency. The second is that automation applied to an inefficient operation will magnify the inefficiency.

—BILL GATES, founder and chairman, Microsoft

Factory work must be adapted to people, not people to machines.

—PEHR G. GYLLENHAMMAR, chairman of the board, MC European Capital S.A., formerly CEO, AB Volvo

Opportunities like [the development of the Mac] don't come along very often. And it's being done by a bunch of people who are incredibly talented but who would be working three levels below the impact of the decisions they're making in this organization…. It won't last forever…. It's more important than their personal lives right now.

—STEVEN JOBS, cofounder and CEO, Apple Computer

Can we design an artificial intelligence that improves upon human discretion for some decisions? I don't know—today. I do know, however, that we will never develop that capacity if we always accept a negative answer, and don't devote the resources necessary to investigate and develop better approaches.

　—T. ALLEN McARTOR, former head, Federal Aviation Agency

What is new is that a class of technicians has managed to remove large data processing expenditures from the control of corporate management and the rule of common sense.

　—RICHARD S. RUBIN, telecommunications manager, Citibank

We try to picture what the product will be and then say, what technology should we be working on today to get us there?

　—JOHN SCULLEY, former chairman, Apple Computer

We found that although we had great technology, we were not translating that technology into value creation in the marketplace. We found we were spending too much money on small incremental projects and not enough on some fundamental breakthroughs.

　—WILLIAM S. STAVROPOULOS, CEO, Dow Chemical

Time Management

Don't say you don't have enough time. You have exactly the same number of hours per day that were given to Helen Keller, Pasteur, Michaelangelo, Mother Teresa, Leonardo da Vinci, Thomas Jefferson, and Albert Einstein.

　—H. JACKSON BROWN, JR., author, *Life's Little Instruction Book*

You will never find time for anything. If you want time you must make it.

 ➤CHARLES BUXTON, English author (1823-1871)

If you ask [people] what percentage of time they are spending on things that are urgent but not important, most would say "Half of the time."

 ➤STEPHEN COVEY, consultant and author, *The 7 Habits of Highly Effective People*

Time is the scarcest resource and unless it is managed nothing else can be managed.

 ➤PETER F. DRUCKER, consultant and renowned management author

From time waste there can be no salvage. It is the easiest of all waste and the hardest to correct because it does not litter the floor.

 HENRY FORD, founder, Ford Motor Company

There's no such thing as not enough time if you're doing what you want to do.

 ➤ROBERT HALF, founder, Robert Half International

The ability to concentrate and to use time well is everything.

 ➤LEE IACOCCA, former chairman, Chrysler Corp.

If a person gets long-winded in explaining something, I say, "Give me the short version." Then I smile, to avoid being perceived as rude.

 ➤STEVE KAHN, CEO, Integrity QA Software

Your hours are your most precious possession. This day is all you have. Waste not a minute.

 ➤OG MANDINO, inspirational speaker and author of several books, including *The Greatest Secret in the World*

Today's innovation is time-based competition.... Give customers what they want when they want it.

—GEORGE STALK, JR. AND THOMAS M. HOUT, authors, *Competing Against Time*

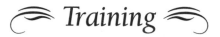

Training

We are forced to rely on people, which is why we put so much emphasis on training.

—HENRY BLOCK, founder, H&R Block

A job in which young people are not given real training—though, of course, the training need not be a formal "training program"— does not measure up to what they have a right and a duty to expect.

—PETER F. DRUCKER, consultant and renowned management author

The five steps in teaching an employee new skills are preparation, explanation, showing, observation and supervision.

—HAROLD HOOK, chairman, American General Insurance Corporation

You can change behavior in an entire organization, provided you treat training as a process rather than as an event.

—EDWARD W. JONES, training director, General Cinema Beverages

If you train people properly, they won't be able to tell a drill from the real thing. If anything, the real thing will be easier.

—RICHARD MARCINKO, CEO, SOS Temps Inc., and best-selling novelist

Train everyone lavishly, you can't overspend on training.

—TOM PETERS, author and consultant

Training, training, retraining, then more training, and if I say it again, then you just don't get it.

—TOM PETERS

Basically the dominant competitive weapon of the 21st century will be the education and skills of the work force
── LESTER THUROW, **former dean, MIT Sloan School of Management**

The mediocre teacher tells. The good teacher explains. The superior teacher demonstrates. The great teacher inspires.
── WILLIAM A. WARD, **former administrator, Texas Wesleyan University**

Women in Business

We never gave up our femininity. We didn't become little men. I don't care to get on equal footing with men.
── JILL BARAD, **former CEO, Mattel**

One of the biggest mistakes women make in business is that they aren't friendly enough.
── CHARLOTTE BEERS, **CEO, J. Walter Thompson**

Competing in a man's world is what I want to do. I'm very much in touch with my male side. I'm really competitive, and I find confrontation stimulating. But I keep those qualities in check. I use my feminine traits—empathy, collaboration.
── NINA DISESA, **chairman, CEO, McCann Erickson**

Being a woman in this job is important. I'm dealing with big egos, big personalities. Fragile, high-maintenance people. If I didn't have a strong nurturing component, I couldn't do it.
── NINA DISESA

Sure, there are barriers at companies that haven't woken up to competition. But at companies competing hard to win every day, there is not a glass ceiling.
── CARLY FIORINA, **chairman and CEO, Hewlett-Packard**

When I was first starting out, I was usually the only woman in the room. And this was a heavy burden, because there was the inevitable moment in the meeting when all these men would turn to me—because we were usually doing advertising to women—and the whole room would turn to me and say, "Well, Shelly, what do women think?" It was extraordinary to speak on the part of all women in the United States. There was a moment of enormous power.

—SHELLY LAZARUS, chairman and CEO, Ogilvy & Mather Advertising

In order to lead in a man's world, you can't be plain vanilla.

—LINDA MARCELLI, director, Merrill Lynch, New York District

Too many women think they can have a wonderful career, a terrific marriage, happy children, and a great social life. It's just not reality.

—REBECCA MARK, CEO, Enron Development

Being superhuman is not possible.... I think women sometimes don't ask for help enough because they feel it is a sign of weakness.

—MAUREEN MCGUIRE, vice president, worldwide marketing communications, IBM

Women's networks do women zero good professionally. My advice is to find a niche and then become the best there is in that field. If you perform, you'll get recognized.

—DARLA MOORE, CEO, Rainwater Inc.

Women are choosing smaller, more flexible companies over traditional ones. Today, more American women work for women-owned businesses than for the *Fortune* 500.

—NANCY RAMSEY, president, Morning Star Imports

These days women are feeling so dispirited about the work world that they're actually leaving their jobs. The so-called glass ceiling isn't the problem. The problem has to do with what women see when they look up at the glass ceiling. They see what they are expected to sacrifice, and they opt out of even trying to smash the glass.

—HELAYNE SPIVAK, former creative director, J. Walter Thompson

About the Editor

John Woods is the president of CWL Publishing Enterprises, a company that develops business books for publishers. He is also the co-author of The McGraw-Hill Encyclopedia of Quality Terms & Concepts and author of The 10-Minute Guide to Teams & Teamwork. He is co-editor of The Quality Yearbook, The ASTD Training and Performance Yearbook, and The Purchasing and Supply Yearbook. All his work incorporates the systems or holistic view of organizations, an approach that in one way or another is captured in the majority of the quotations included in this book. You can learn more about John and CWL Publishing Enterprises at his Web site, www.cwlpub.com.